POETRY COMPE

CW00602174

GREAT MINDS

Your World...Your Future...YOUR WORDS

- Inspirations From
The Midlands Vol II
Edited by Aimée Vanstone

 Young**Writers**

First published in Great Britain in 2005 by:
Young Writers
Remus House
Coltsfoot Drive
Peterborough
PE2 9JX
Telephone: 01733 890066
Website: www.youngwriters.co.uk

SB ISBN 1 84602 293 2

Foreword

This year, the Young Writers' 'Great Minds' competition proudly presents a showcase of the best poetic talent selected from over 40,000 up-and-coming writers nationwide.

Young Writers was established in 1991 to promote the reading and writing of poetry within schools and to the youth of today. Our books nurture and inspire confidence in the ability of young writers and provide a snapshot of poems written in schools and at home by budding poets of the future.

The thought, effort, imagination and hard work put into each poem impressed us all and the task of selecting poems was a difficult but nevertheless enjoyable experience.

We hope you are as pleased as we are with the final selection and that you and your family continue to be entertained with *Great Minds - Inspirations From The Midlands Vol II* for many years to come.

Contents

Alderman Smith School, Nuneaton

Amy Gadsby (14)   24
Charlie Towle (12)   24
Clayton Harper (12)   25
Ellie Hoverd (14)   25
Paige Stewart & Gemma Wood (14)   26
Georgina Lloyd (11)   26
Lydia Wren (14)   27
Taylor Robinson (12)   27
Ella Mallabone (14)   28
Jamie Galland (14)   28
Megan Roberts (14)   29
Matthew Clark (14)   29
Denise Myers (14)   30
Craig Barnes (13)   30
Kenny Kay (14)   31
Lauren Bentley (14)   31
Melanie Gunn (14)   32
Danielle Worthington (14)   33
Daniella Deeming (11)   34
Julia Blyth (14)   35
Kira Sharp (12)   36
Stephanie Johnson (14)   37
Alex Jones (14)   37
Gabriella Robinson (13)   38

Archbishop Grimshaw School, Chelmsley Wood
John Cooke (14)   38
Samantha Perry (14)   39
Brenda Kane (14)   39
Brett Mannion (14)   40
Christine O'Reilly (11)   40
Mark Mulvihill (14)   41
Kimberley Moloney (13)   42
Terri Evans (14)   42
Laura Price (15)   43
Tiffany Chatterley (14)   43
Jodie Phillips (14)   44
Jordan Hay (12)   44
Kate Eaton (14)   45
Thomas Bruce (14)   45
Lisa Barrett (13)   46

Ryan Chapman (12)   46
Ryan Hewitt (12)   47
Bruce Shingler (13)   47
Aiden Sartin (11)   48
Claire Myatt (12)   48
Daniel Ryan   49
Nathan Kelly (12)   49
Chris Bounds (12) & Mitchell Joy   50
Shannon Knight (12)   51
Lucy Woodcock (12)   51
Helen Keane (12)   52
Victoria Ireland (13)   53
Tinekka-Jade Pascoe (12)   53
Maisie Parry (14)   54
James Jones-Styzaker (14)   54
Perry Nash (12)   55
Sarah Grice (14)   55
Kyle Fennell (12)   56
Natasha Dickenson (12)   56
Dannielle Brickley (14)   57
Kellie Light & Kirsty Jackson (12)   57
Danielle Billingsley (13)   58
Joel Mallabar (12)   58
Amy Masters (13)   58
Ryan Muldowney (12)   59

Ash Green School, Ash Green
Jamie Hewitt (12)   59
Selina Chauhan (14)   60
Lewis Jones (12)   61
Courtney Hastie   61
Paige Barratt (12)   62
Hollie Docker (12)   63
Lewis Morris (12)   64
Beth Calcott (12)   65
Steven Davies (12)   66
Andrew Walker (12)   67
Stevie Roberts (13)   68
Rosie Wood (11)   68
James Townsley   69
Shannon Kincade (11)   70

Namrata Bhardwaj (11)   71
Paula Sears (12)   72
Chelsee-Jade Hollihead (12)   73

Bigwood Secondary School, Warren Hill

Abigail Spencer (13)   73
Onome Abara (13)   74
Kristie Butler (13)   74
Lee Sykes (13)   75
Romy Idle (13)   76
Terri Charles (13)   76
Ashley Warsop (13)   77
Maciey Freestone-McDonald (13)   77
Peter Revill (12)   78
Lauren Chambers (13)   78
Sophie Barker (13)   79
Penny Waltham (13)   79
Lucy Williams (12)   80
Niamh Hickey (13)   80
Melissa Blake (13)   81
Jennie Wallace (13)   81
Rochelle Freestone-McDonald (13)   82
Wain Marriott (13)   82
Jenna Shipman (14)   83
Charlotte Haywood (13)   83
Ashley Shepherd (13)   84
Katie McEvoy (13)   85
Sean Duryea (13)   85
Mark Thornton (13)   86
Rebecca Sabin (13)   86
Nathan Judge (13)   86
Rebecca Armes (13)   87
Shannen Naylor (13)   87
Jamie McGougan (13)   87
Adam Robinson (13)   88
Luke Butler (13)   88
Jodie Sturman (13)   88
Samantha Swinscoe (13)   89
Luke Waine (13)   89
Ashley Whitehead (13)   89

Caludon Castle Business and Enterprise Specialist School, Wyken

Heather Auckland (12)	90
Beth Cain (11)	90
Diviyen Mistry (12)	91
Siân Lucas (13)	91
Lauren McDonell (12)	92
Lewis O'Brien (13)	92
Charley-Rose Borgeat (12)	93
Bethany McKenna (12)	93
Sophie Stuart (13)	94
Liam Mistry (11)	94
Jade Horgan (13)	95
Laura Wedgbury (12)	95
Stanley Saungweme (12)	96
Navraj Chahal (11)	96
Leigh Bell	97
Chloe Evatt (12)	97
Iknam Chaven (11)	97
Steven Cotton (11) & Arranvir Dosanjh (12)	98
Perri McMahon (12)	98

Churnet View Middle School, Leek

Dominic Dutton (13)	98
Lisa Marie Payne (13)	99
Holly Bailey (13)	99
Jasmine Moss (13)	99
Matthew Smart (12)	100
Tracy Drury (13)	100
Leanne Sales (13)	101
Daniel Austin (13)	101
Stephanie Robinson (13)	102
Kayleigh Barber (12)	102
Jamie Duffield (12)	103
Lyndon Birks (13)	103
Amy Condrey (13)	104
Ben Johnson (13)	104
Liam Dukesell (13)	105
Lee Boswell (13)	105
Amy Corden (13)	106
Max Yapp (13)	106

Elliott Goldstraw (13)   107
Ryan Burkitt (13)   107

Derby High School, Littleover
Rebecca Thomas (14)   108
Leah Beardmore (14)   109
Lauren Bond (14)   110
Daisy Williams (14)   111
Rebecca Bussey (14)   112
Lizzie Saunders (14)   113

Four Dwellings High School, Quinton
Niki Thomas (12)   113
Alisha Myatt (13)   114
Paul Cashmore (12)   115
Michelle Pike (13)   115
Maisy Moran (12)   116
Tristan Dyas (13)   117
Rosie Dawes (12)   118
Jake Moroney (12)   119

Hagley Park Sports College, Rugeley
Matthew Jackson (12)   119
Lorna Chilton (15)   120
Rob Earle (15)   120
Kevin Guy (15)   121
Sam Gunby (15)   121
Alan Malpass (15)   122
Michelle Whitty (15)   123
Yasmin Follows (14)   124
Charlotte Blackford (14)   125
Daniel Pyatt (15)   126
Ryan Hicks (14)   127

Haywood School, Sherwood
Ayla Smythe (14)   127
Elisha Edwards (14)   128
Claire Johnson (13)   129
Jade Hoppis (14)   130

King Edward VI Camp Hill School For Girls, Kings Heath

Marcella Meehan (12)	153
Shivangee Maurya (12)	154
Crystal Griffiths (12)	154
Heather Phoenix (12)	155
Nyasha Zvobgo (11)	155
Neha Sandhu (12)	156
Saaira Mushtaq (12)	156
Jo Richards (12)	157
Emma Crighton (12)	158
Eleanor Russell (12)	159

Lady Hawkins' School, Kington

Daniel Edwards (14)	159
Matthew Filbrandt (13)	160
Olivia Coppock (13)	160
Kizmet Nibbs (13)	161
Daniel Owens (14)	161
Jasmine Evans (13)	162
George Watson (13)	163
Sophie Jones (13)	164
Kelly Owen (14)	165
Kathryn McKenna (15)	166
Piran Treen (15)	167
Matthew Lampitt (13)	168
Joanne Allford (13)	169
Ellen Baines (13)	170
James Gardiner (18)	171
Dominic Barnes (14)	172

Littleover Community School, Derby

Hannah Foxon (13)	172
Katie Bradford (13)	173
Laura Hewitson (13)	173
Jennifer Unwin (13)	174
Sarah Taylor (13)	175
Harkiran Sagoo (14)	176
Anita Ghei (13)	177
Matthew Sheffield (13)	

Lordswood Girls' School, Harborne

Keshia Russell (12)	178
Eleanor Mason (12)	179
Nosheen Tabassum (12)	180
Sunaina Deol (12)	181
Divya Rani (12)	182
Elizabeth Sinton (11)	183
Candice Edwards (12)	184
Sahila Khanum (12)	185
Monica Chirrimar (12)	186
Gaganjit Sandhu (12)	187
Jillian Alger (13)	188
Simerpreet Sanghera (12)	189
Munira Muflehi (11)	190
Jasdeep Kandola (12)	191

Moseley Park School, Bilston

Becky Shirley (13)	191
Leena Patel (13)	192
Lee Potts (13)	193
Samantha Pritchard (15)	193
Whitney Barton (12)	194
Stephen Bayliss (13)	194
Natalie Wolverson (13)	195
Katherine Owen (13)	195
Lauren Field (13)	196
Raja Clair (15)	196
Vinod Birdi (13) & Tia Rafferty (13)	197
Kayleigh Evans (13)	197
Jade Davis (15)	198
Hayley Bate (15)	199
Chris Bray (15)	200
Jagdeep Sandhu (13)	200
Rebekah O'Neil (15)	201
Siobhan Codner (15)	201
Monica Patel (17)	202
Samantha Turner (17)	202
Natalie Sheargold (15)	203
Catherine Holmes (16)	203
Katie Dudwell (15)	204
Samantha Baker (17)	205

The Poems

Letting Go

At times I lay awake at night,
I used to sit and cry.
Whenever I saw happiness,
I watched it pass me by.

You always loomed right over me,
A shadow to block my soul.
I thought there would be no escape,
From life, this great black hole.

I craved so dearly to get away,
And my work is paying off.
I see light at the end of the tunnel,
And I've stopped hearing your laugh

You thought that I would never be free,
I'll admit, progress was slow.
But I deceived you with my heart,
And I'm finally letting go.

Helen Reed (13)
Alderman Smith School, Nuneaton

Nurse

I am a nurse today, a doctor tomorrow
I heal your hurt, upset and sorrow
I come to you at night
When you're ill and white.
You normally go out healthy and alright
Thanks to me staying up all night.
When I go home, my work is not done
I am rushed off my feet 'cause I run and run
And the best part of the day is when
I curl up in bed with a nurse at my side
Tending to m
y aching head.

Emma Biddle (13)
Alderman Smith School, Nuneaton

They Are Horrid

They are *horrid*
They bully me
They are *horrid*
They hurt me
They hit me
And take my money off me
They are *horrid*
They pull my hair
They kick me
They strangle me
Why . . . ? Why . . . ? Why . . . ?
They are *horrid*
Maybe 'cause they're angry
Maybe 'cause they're sad
Why . . . ? Why . . . ? Why . . . ?
It's always me
I hate my life
They are *horrid*
Why . . . ? Why . . . ? Why . . . ?
I know what they are
They are *horrid*.

Stacey Merry (12)
Alderman Smith School, Nuneaton

Grandad's Car

Rattle, hum, hiss, bang,
This car has got to go!
It really is quite sick
It huffs and puffs and blows!

Crackle, whizz, cough, wheeze,
I think it's going to stop!
We've just gone round a corner,
And the engine's fallen right off!

Rory Smith (13)
Alderman Smith School, Nuneaton

My Darling Wife

To my darling wife,
Don't worry about me,
I'm still alive,
Well, my soul is you see.
I'll sit up in Heaven
And watch over you,
Because my darling wife,
I still love you.

I'll help you through sadness
Keep the tears away,
I'll keep you happy,
Every night and every day.
Keep me in your heart,
And remember me,
'Cause when you pass away
You'll be up here with me.

In Heaven I will,
Fill you with love
You'll be like this, all ready
In the land up above.

So my darling,
Don't worry about me
I'm still alive
Well, my soul is you see
I'll sit up in Heaven
And watch over you
Because my darling wife
I still love you.

Connor Miller (13)
Alderman Smith School, Nuneaton

The Cat In The Six Stages Of Life

(Inspired by 'As You Like It' by William Shakespeare)

First is when she was born,
Not ever wanting to mourn,
My mother said to me,
Go and clean that cat or she will catch a flea.

Then she was older and her mother died,
I could not comfort her, all I did was cried,
She was only two months old,
When I held her, she felt cold.

When I was eight,
She slid under the gate,
I was very upset,
And it was her I went to get.

Now she is older,
I am getting bolder,
She is now eleven,
And I am twenty-seven.

Now she is ill,
She has to have a pill,
I am at work all day,
We have no time to play.

She is now dying,
All I am doing is crying,
She will die,
As time passes by.

Charlene Readman (12)
Alderman Smith School, Nuneaton

Boys

Boys are stupid
Boys do play
I hate them more every day,
They break your heart,
And make you cry
But worst of all
They always lie.
Boys say 'I love you'
Then say it's 'poo'
But when you leave them
It somehow becomes true.
In the end you're not an ex,
Cos all boys know is how to say,
Next!
You can never forget the sweet,
Kind and caring guys
That never come near.
But if they do,
They're bound to sneer!

Kirsty Shaw (14)
Alderman Smith School, Nuneaton

My Dog

My dog is brown and hairy
And is soft and cute
He sometimes can be scary
But often he's astute.

He reminds me of a teddy bear
So snug and warm to cuddle
To love and feed and take good care of
But causes such a muddle!

Natasha Penny (13)
Alderman Smith School, Nuneaton

The First Time I Scored A Goal!

I always wanted to know what it felt like
To score a goal when watching
Football on the TV.
They made it look so easy
But I could never do it.
I tried so hard but it never happened.
My dad always said I could,
'Do it,' my brother said.
'Whack it,' the others told me to place it
So I whacked it
But at the same time I placed it
And the keeper had no chance.
Then all the hairs on my back froze
My body started shaking . . .
I'm the goal-scoring king!

Daniel Young (12)
Alderman Smith School, Nuneaton

In The Morning

Mum is wailing from the stairs
Sis is sleeping on the chairs.
Brother asleep till 8 o'clock,
Dad trying to sleep, so counting the flock.
I'm in the bathroom for an hour,
Knocks on the door, 'I want a shower.'
We rush to the car to get the front seat,
Like animals racing for the meat.
Then we get to school,
And my sister starts to drool,
There's the boy that she likes,
My brother will get into fights,
And that's what happens in the morning!

Becki Whiston (13)
Alderman Smith School, Nuneaton

Beauty Is . . .

Beauty is . . .
A bunch of flowers,
Smelling nice and fresh,
Beauty is . . .
A box of chocolates,
Delicious and sweet,
Beauty is . . .
Like a rainbow,
Coloured and wonderful,
Beauty is . . .
A newborn baby,
Little and so sweet,
Beauty is . . .
The summer's sun,
Shining brightly in the sky,
Beauty is . . .
A starry night,
Sparkly with the moonlight beams,
Beauty is . . .
Everything,
You and me,
Everyone in sight.

Katie Berry (13) & Katie Jones (14)
Alderman Smith School, Nuneaton

Dolphin

D is for dolphin, dancing in the sun
O is for ocean, that's where they live
L is for lovely, that's what they are
P is for playful, they're better than anyone else
H is for helping other dolphins in need
I is for intelligence, cleverer than me
N is for noble, the leader of the gang.

Danielle Timson (13)
Alderman Smith School, Nuneaton

Terrorist Attacks

These terrorist wars do not solve anything
I mean, take the Twin Towers in America
They had no reason, just destroyed the place
Picture in your mind the bombs going off
Panic!
People running and screaming
Crying small children would have been so frightened
We only saw it on TV
Like watching a video tape
But people who saw it happen have to live with it
Seeing the plane going into the middle of the two buildings
Now it's the UK
London city on trains and buses
Lives destroyed, people missing, injured
They will not win or make us give in
These evil terrorists
It makes us stronger
As we carry on with our lives
Stand as we have before in times of war.

Joseph Sadler (13)
Alderman Smith School, Nuneaton

Beauty Is . . .

Beauty is many things in this world
The only thing that matters is what's inside
Beauty is bright and colourful
Like a flower growing in the spring
Beauty is looking nice
Beauty is smelling nice
Beauty is anything you want it to be
It doesn't matter what you look like
You will always be beautiful.

Beauty is . . .

Katie Brain (14)
Alderman Smith School, Nuneaton

They Are Bullies

They call me names,
They pull my hair,
They trip me up,
They laugh and stare,
They are a pack of hyenas,
They laugh at anything,
They pick on me and hit me,
They make up things to sing,
They are nasty and horrible.

They pick on me
Because they think they're strong and tough,
They think they can pick on me because
They think I'm weak,
But I know what they really are,
They are bullies.

Richard Payne (13)
Alderman Smith School, Nuneaton

Beauty Is . . .

Beauty is so cool
It fills your life like a pool
Beauty is like a puppy-dog
It's like a great big snog
Beauty is so full of flowers
It fills your life with a wonderful smell
Beauty is like a rainbow
It's like the sparkling sky
Beauty is so wonderful
It is like the whole wide world.

Gurminder Kaur (14)
Alderman Smith School, Nuneaton

Empty

The pale moon bare,
I'm turning to despair.
Crying, I clench my fist,
I take the cold blade to my wrist.

Taking a deep breath,
Hoping at last, this will be my death.
Tears running down my face,
Now I have fallen from grace.

Dragging the blade across my arm,
Why isn't it doing any harm?
Slowly the blood trickles out cold,
Now I know I'll never grow old.

I make the wounds deeper,
Now I'm starting to feel weaker.
I drop the letter onto the bed,
Explaining to my family why I'm dead.

I whisper his name,
Hoping one day he'll do the same.
For someone who said they loved me,
You hurt me,
And now I'm free . . .

Danielle Palmer (13)
Alderman Smith School, Nuneaton

Beauty

Beauty can be on the inside and out.
Beauty is like a bunch of flowers.
Beauty is like a box of chocolates.
Beauty is like a rainbow.
Beauty is like a little baby.
Beauty is everyone and everything.

Paul Simpson (14)
Alderman Smith School, Nuneaton

Beauty Is . . .

Beauty is nature, the flowers and the trees.
Beauty is seeing your family every day
And seeing the smiles on their faces
And your friends and other people.

Only you can make beauty
No one else can make it for you.
Beauty is you.

Beauty is the special events that take place,
Like the newborn baby holding your hand,
Gurgling at you.
Beauty is the animals, your pets and life.

Beauty comes from inside you,
It doesn't matter what you look like on the outside,
It's the inside that counts.
Beauty is your friends that are always there for you,
And when you are happy.

But always remember this,
Beauty is you.

Stacey Silverwood (14)
Alderman Smith School, Nuneaton

Beauty

Beauty is an amazing thing
Makes you feel just like a king

It takes a while to find
Some people get left behind

It's somewhere inside
Somewhere in the hide.

Keep looking for it
You'll find it some day.

Michael Watson (13)
Alderman Smith School, Nuneaton

Beauty

Beauty is like a flower flowering in springtime
Watching your family growing up

Beauty is dressing up
Make-up
The way you have your hair.

Beauty is . . .
Beauty is something you can't describe

Beauty is skin-deep
Only you know what your true beauty is

Your beauty is inside
Inside everyone
Only you know your true beauty

Beauty is
You.

Elaine Hall (14)
Alderman Smith School, Nuneaton

Softly

Softly the cat jumped on the bed,
Softly the boy lay down his head,
Softly the girl picked up the baby,
Softly the tiger crept up on the lady.

Softly the feather landed on the floor,
Softly the little boy said,
'May I have more?'
Softly the wind whistled
Through the trees,
Softly the mouse nibbled at the cheese!

Sami Ryder (12)
Alderman Smith School, Nuneaton

Drayton Manor

Drayton Manor is really great,
We went around with all our mates.

First we went on Stormforce 10,
When we got off we went on again.

The Buffalo ride curled our toes.
We then went on for another four goes.

Next we looked at Apocalypse,
But Taylor's tummy felt a bit sick.

Black Revolver was dark and loud,
When the music came on, we couldn't hear a sound.

Siân wanted to go on Maelstrom,
But Taylor said, 'No, because of my tum.'

We then went to get signed in,
And gave Miss Williamson a cheeky grin.

Splash Canyon was full of jokes,
When they pulled them, we all got soaked.

When we got back on the coach,
We ate our sandwiches and Siân nearly choked.

Thank you for listening to our Drayton Manor poem,
Maybe one day you would like to go in.

Siân Jones & Taylor Robinson (11)
Alderman Smith School, Nuneaton

The Wendigo Imitation

(Based on 'The Wendigo' by Ogden Nash)

The Nastyo,
The Nastyo,
Its skin is coarse and floppyo,
Its eyes are blue and blinky,
Its mouth is wide and pinky,
Its nose is big and snotty, you know,
I saw it just a week ago,
It's hungry,
It's smelly,
It's got a big wobbly belly
I see it on the telly,
I find it in my welly,
It will eat you up,
And drink your blood,
It's coming to get you.

Kelsey Varden (12)
Alderman Smith School, Nuneaton

Beauty Is

Beauty is many different things
Beauty can be what you look like
Or what you may see.

Beauty can be flowers
Beauty can be looks
The best beauty is inside of you.

Beauty doesn't always matter
The looks or what you may see
Just remember the beauty inside of you
That's the beauty that counts.

Louise Lomas (14)
Alderman Smith School, Nuneaton

Sorry

My life is pointless
I've lost all happiness
No one can help
However hard I scream and yelp
I've been betrayed again
Why did you mention my name?
I've got feelings too
I'm not some rubbish stuck to your shoe
I may be shy
But it doesn't mean I don't cry
Why should I laugh when they take my stuff?
I've had enough
You wanted to know why I'm unhappy and sad
Well it's not because I'm going mad
It's because the world is so unfair
And no one seems to care
So thank you for showing your concern
And for helping me learn
I'm sorry that you had to read this
But thank you Miss!

Charlotte Hall (14)
Alderman Smith School, Nuneaton

Beauty Is

Beauty is smelling nice
Beauty is looking nice
No matter how nice you look
It's inside where your
Beauty is.
Beauty is having fun
Beauty is like a lovely flower
Smells and looks
Nice every single . . . day.

Kelly-Ann Robinson (14)
Alderman Smith School, Nuneaton

Brand New Automatic Daffodils

(Based on 'I WanderedLlonely as a Cloud' by William Wordsworth)

I wandered lonely as a bottle of Clinique
'That floats on high over vales and hills',
When all at once advanced stop signs
A host of very improved anti-ageing creams
Beside the lake, targets lines, dark spots
'Fluttering and dancing in the breeze'.

'Continuous as the stars that shine'
And twinkle, vanish the look of lines.
They stretched in never-ending lines
Along the 100% fragrance free
'Ten thousand saw I at a glance'
Tossing their heads at targets, lines and dark spots
A dark spot for a more even skin tone.

Poppy Turner, Chantelle Albrighton & Melissa Pratt (13)
Alderman Smith School, Nuneaton

The New Automatic Daffodils

(Based on 'I Wandered Lonely as a Cloud' by William Wordsworth)

'I wandered lonely as a cloud'
Time, perfection can make you look younger
It isn't easy to dance to one sound
I record your new, in-depth forecast
And it can do nothing but good
'Continuous as the stars that shine'
And twinkle in the night's sky.
You can make a connection between two worlds
But only if you use Imedeen
Inner strength and outer beauty
They flash upon the inward eye
If you do this you will see
You will find the inner beauty of Imedeen.

Kelly Wright & Jack Bingham (13)
Alderman Smith School, Nuneaton

School Days (The Happiest Days Of Your Life?)

My school holidays are going to be great
I'm going to watch TV and stay up late.
I just can't wait
I'm going to hang out with my mates.
School is out
My mates and me will give a shout.

The uniform can hang on the door
Those boring lessons are no more.
I can read my books and eat when I like
And I can put my hair in coloured spikes.

When all my school years are done
I'm looking forward to having fun.
But really in reality
It will be hard out there finding a job for me.

It's a 'rat race' in the 'big wide world'
Finding my future all alone.
It seemed so simple then but now,
How do I take charge and plan the rest of my life?

Jordan Handley (14)
Alderman Smith School, Nuneaton

Last Breath

We were being chased down an alleyway,
My boyfriend and me,
Being chased by a gang with guns.
Three deafening shots were heard,
Then silence.
My boyfriend fell to the floor,
Three bullet wounds to his head.
His last kiss the longest,
His last breath the shortest,
The last kiss,
The last breath,
I let him slip away.

Amy Rose (13)
Alderman Smith School, Nuneaton

An African Elephant's Life

(Inspired by 'As You Like It' by William Shakespeare)

The precious elephant enters the world
The small, innocent infant,
Stares into its mother's eyes
He lays, helpless,
Like an injured soldier.

Time to be responsible
He's growing up
His beautiful ivory trunks now have reached 10 kgs
His flexible trunk is gathering food
The baby elephant is no longer small.

Now a leader of the herd
What was a child,
Is now an adult
Wiser and stronger
As he explores the Savannah grasslands.

The African elephant has young of its own,
He leads a good example for his young,
And the young of many others
He tries to protect them from hunters and killers
To stop the population going down.

He's now become old,
Weaker and tired
His grey skin more wrinkled than ever before
And his 6000 kg body slowly mingles with the new.

Just like the beginning, weak and helpless
His body slows down,
What was a large, beautiful elephant,
Is now passing away
He lays there thinking,
And then takes one last breath.

Naiomi Howley (12)
Alderman Smith School, Nuneaton

The Fearsome Lion!

(Inspired by 'Jabberwocky' by Lewis Carrol)

T'was evening and the rustling reeds,
Did sway and shimmer in the breeze;
All silent were the animals,
And the night grew peaceful.

Beware the lions, my son,
The jaws that gash, the claws that clash!
Shun the hawk and elude,
The slinking puma of the lands!

And through the woods did he seek,
His elusive opponent from afar,
As one day he sat upon a tree,
The beam from glowing, sickly, yellow eyes shone!

As he drew the gleaming, golden sword from its sheath
The mighty beast thrust forwards!
Swish! Swish! The severed head was to be found,
In a swirling pool of deep blood!
And our hero strode home.

Upon sight, crowds gathered as the father pushed
A question - 'Has thou slain the lion?'
'Hooray! Run to my embrace, my darling boy!
The offspring of this land, owe to you eternal thanks!'

Our hero is gone now,
His skeleton turned to dust.
Yet the people still salute him.
As the slayer of the macabre lion!
He lives on.

David Foster (12)
Alderman Smith School, Nuneaton

Turtle

(Inspired by 'As You Like It' by William Shakespeare)

At first the egg,
Hidden deep in the sand,
With all the other eggs,
With no helping hand.

And then the baby,
At last being able to see,
Trying to scramble down the beach,
To reach the edge of the sea.

And then the youngster,
Learning to find her feet,
Swimming around and finding food,
But avoiding being fresh meat.

And then the adult,
Finding and catching her prey,
Meeting other turtles,
And getting stronger every day.

And then she mates,
She's going away,
Back to the beach,
For she has eggs to lay.

And then growing old,
But still getting larger,
She's not the strongest anymore,
Because other turtles can barge her.

And then she dies,
She's had a good life you see,
She's done well to live to this age,
But now she'll make a nice tea.

Gareth Burdon (12)
Alderman Smith School, Nuneaton

Save Me

I look for help in the light
So it can save me
My life is starting to be a fight
It might give me the key
To the gates of Heaven
Surely this will save me
If I get a little help from He,
He who is our Lord
He'll save me from this pain
If He draws His sword
And cuts the chain
That holds me back
The chains now feel slack
Now I don't feel sick
Nor being hit with a stick
I can breathe again
I can see the light
Now I don't have to fight
Cos He has saved me.

Josh Brown (13)
Alderman Smith School, Nuneaton

Beauty Is . . .

Beauty is a rainbow in the sky
Beauty is a newborn baby
Beauty is a lovely smell
Beauty is a golden ring
Beauty is a starry night
Beauty is a sunset
Beauty is a sparkling sea
Beauty is a wonderful breeze.

Natasha Young (13)
Alderman Smith School, Nuneaton

The Dogigo!

(Based on 'Jabberwocky' by Lewis Carrol)

T'was draughty and the swaying trees,
Did shake and rustle in the night,
All exhausted were the birds
And the clouds' reign ended.

'Beware the Dogigo my son!
The tail that lashes, the eye that blinds,
Beware of the Falcon, and also
The Cloudy Bodysnatcher.'

He took his legendary sword in hand,
Long time the immortal foe he sought,
So rested by the apple trees
And stood in thought.

And as in a coincidental thought he stood,
The Dogigo, with ears on point,
Came slithering through the wicked woods
And gurgled as he came.

One, two, one, two!
And between and between
The legendary sword in hand went *phhhhh!*
He left it dead with its tails
He went skipping back.

And I have slayed the Dogigo
Come to my arms, my shining boy
Oh what a fabulous day, *hallelujah! Hurrah!*
He choked in joy.

Daniel Hollis (12)
Alderman Smith School, Nuneaton

This Is Me!

My life was happy,
Once upon a time,
My life isn't right,
It feels like a mime.

I get called gay
What is wrong with that?
I also get called
A boff, a goth and fat.

I can't keep it all in,
I have to let it all out,
Am I mad because
I like to shout?

Friends aren't my life,
I have interests too.
They look at us, we know,
They haven't got a clue.

What is ordinary?
What is normal?
When I go out,
I dress up formal.

This is my life
Not how I wanted it to be,
I'm not gonna change,
This is me!

Ceri Morris (14)
Alderman Smith School, Nuneaton

No Regrets

I see a boy I really like
But I coop it up inside,
He asks me out,
What shall I say?
I love him but I don't,
I hardly know him, what do I do?
Who am I to tell?
A best friend, a parent or sister?
Who can I confide in?
I should say yes,
It's a flying guess,
But two months later I don't regret.
We see each other every week,
But the time comes once again,
When I have to let him go.
Once again,
Just another week . . .

Amy Gadsby (14)
Alderman Smith School, Nuneaton

My Mum

She's as brainy as a calculator
She's like a big soft pillow
She's as comforting as a bed
She's as warm as a just-lit candle
She's as helpful as a TV remote
She's as loyal as a fridge freezer
She's as loving as a big teddy bear
She's as kind as a big armchair
She's as cheerful as a big vase of fresh flowers
She's my mum!

Charlie Towle (12)
Alderman Smith School, Nuneaton

The Wendigo Recreated

(Based on 'The Wendigo' by Ogden Nash)

The Sevigoose,
The Sevigoose!
Its horns are big like a moose!
Its face is like a huge square,
Its body is covered in hair.
Its poison lingers if you touch it,
And if you do, you will regret it!

The Sevigoose,
The Sevigoose!
It's not likely to let you loose,
But when it's grabbed you, get away,
Or you won't live another day!

Clayton Harper (12)
Alderman Smith School, Nuneaton

Daddy's Lil Girl

Born I was,
12th May
My daddy spoke and said, 'Hey'.
Said I was beautiful,
I'll always be there,
He really did care.
Mummy had gone,
Couldn't take the pain,
Didn't hear my first word,
Didn't see my first tear,
Didn't feel my first teddy bear,
Daddy was there,
He really did care,
Here I am, twenty years on,
My heart is throbbing,
Now Daddy has gone.

Ellie Hoverd (14)
Alderman Smith School, Nuneaton

A Family Of Five

There's one special guy I truly love
He was sent to me from the heavens above
He made my wishes and dreams come true
When he asked me to marry him, I said, 'I do!'

Now we're married and living together,
We're now a proud mother and father
The years have passed
The children have grown,
Now packing and ready to leave home.

We got what we wanted, a family of five
Living together in this home of pride
We all love each other so very much
Hoping that we stay in touch.

Mummy and Daddy have gone now kids
We send you all our one last kiss
We'll be watching over you from the heavens above
So take care kids and remember, be good.

Paige Stewart & Gemma Wood (14)
Alderman Smith School, Nuneaton

Gently And Lovingly

Gently the mother touches your arm,
Gently the dancer leaps in the air,
Gently the dog sniffs your palm,
Gently the breeze ruffles your hair.

Lovingly she hugs her son,
Lovingly she strokes her dog,
Lovingly she warms her home,
But the most loving thing she could ever do,
Is be herself all year through.

Georgina Lloyd (11)
Alderman Smith School, Nuneaton

Farewell

I'm not there as the sun rises
I see the tears that fill your eyes
I hate to see you like this my dear
And so down my face runs a single tear
I will always be with you my love
So every time you see a dove
I want you to remember me
The dove is a gift from me you'll see
I never thought this day would come
When I would leave a ghastly sum
Things that I would miss the most
More than your famous roast
It's you my love I'll miss and miss
Wasn't it so sweet, our final kiss.
I'll say farewell 'cause I'm up in Heaven
I'm watching them twenty-four-seven
I want to say my final goodbye
Don't worry now, don't even sigh,
I'm as happy as can be
When you come to me you'll see
Down my face runs a final tear
I love you so much, my faithful dear.

Lydia Wren (14)
Alderman Smith School, Nuneaton

Quickly

Quickly all the waves come in and out
Quickly all the children run about,
Quickly all the clouds come in,
Quickly blood is pouring out of his chin.

Quickly all the cars go by,
Quickly aeroplanes fly in the sky,
Quickly an ambulance goes,
Quickly the wind blows.

Taylor Robinson (12)
Alderman Smith School, Nuneaton

A Lonely Life

On the 8th July 1991,
A woman walks into her house
A baby in her arms
A pram in the kitchen
No man there anymore
The sound of the birds has suddenly died out
A sad moment for us all
To think this happened fourteen years ago
Stands out very small
But life goes on, a lonely life
For mother and child alone
Through the years there are laughs and tears
And a heavy drone of whispers at night
A very bad fright, the girl jumps in her skin
Only mother and child forever a lonely life
For them both together . . .

Ella Mallabone (14)
Alderman Smith School, Nuneaton

Skating . . .

When I put on my skates
I get a good feeling
Jump from the ground
And nearly hit the ceiling.
I skate out of the house,
And don't make a sound,
Jump onto the ramps
A new trick I have found.
I skate down town,
And jump down steps,
Pull a few spins
It's a real big test!

Jamie Galland (14)
Alderman Smith School, Nuneaton

Beauty Is . . .

Beauty is in winter
Rocks and soil
It lies in babies
Young and old to see the world
The story untold
Beauty lies in flowers
Roses, lilies and daffodils
Beauty, beauty . . .

Ugliness is . . .
Ugliness is nothing
It snows on no living thing
Everyone's lovely, no one's ugly

It doesn't matter who you are
You're never ugly.

Megan Roberts (14)
Alderman Smith School, Nuneaton

A Fiery End

As I stare down
Into a fiery hole,
The fire is on me,
Stop, drop, roll!

I'm staring now into,
A massive inferno,
The oxygen feeding it,
Making it grow!

I cannot get out,
I know this for sure
So I grab a knife,
And slit my throat by the door!

Matthew Clark (14)
Alderman Smith School, Nuneaton

The Dream

The biggest day of my life
I'm shaking like a leaf
Thoughts in my head telling me to 'breathe'.
As I walk up the aisle
People stare in amazement,
This feels like the longest walk of my life.

I stand there, deeply scared,
In case I mess things up,
The words flow straight from my heart,
Telling him how much I love him
I gaze deeply into his ocean-blue eyes
Feeling that I have found 'the one'.

As the words flow from his mouth
I stand in amazement at how he truly feels,
As the ring slips onto my sweaty finger,
My dream is complete.

Everything that I have ever wanted
Is standing right in front of me
And it is sealed with a kiss
This is the happiest day of my life.

Denise Myers (14)
Alderman Smith School, Nuneaton

My Brother

I have a little brother,
There really is no other.
His front two teeth are missin',
Dad says 'Too much kissin'.'
He's a cheeky little man,
And helps out when he can.
But what is really great,
Is that he is my best mate!

Craig Barnes (13)
Alderman Smith School, Nuneaton

Air Force Combat

Aeroplanes flying in the air
Being navigated from the ground
People below just stand and stare
How much they outstand.

Loop-the-loop
A barrel roll
Troop to troop
Through little holes.

How amazing they really are
Even in combat
They go far, far, far.

This is my future
It's what I want to be
A pilot in the RAF
Soon it will be me.

Kenny Kay (14)
Alderman Smith School, Nuneaton

Baby Girl

Happiness is a baby girl,
A great big smile,
A treasured girl,
Hugs and kisses,
Laughter, cries,
Bedtime stories,
Lullabies,
The sweetest gift
You could possess,
A baby girl is happiness!

Lauren Bentley (14)
Alderman Smith School, Nuneaton

Love

Love is a new baby,
So sweet, new and pure,
It's a picture, a painting,
The ocean, the shore.

Love is beauty,
That is more than skin deep
It's a promise, a gift,
A present to keep.

Love is a lift,
When you can't walk
It's hope, trust, friendship,
A serious talk.

Love is a sister,
A dad, a cousin, a mother.
It's an aunty, an uncle,
A grandma, a brother.

Love is a puzzle
A mystery, a dream,
It's a pocket of happiness,
That is not all it seems.

Love is a structure,
Full of protection,
It's courage, power,
Joy and affection.

Love is the base
Of all mankind,
Through all stages of life,
This is love we may find.

Melanie Gunn (14)
Alderman Smith School, Nuneaton

Sounds Of Suicide

Your blood runs cold
Through your veins,
Screams so loud,
Sounds of suicide.

Dripping blood,
Tearful eyes,
Screams burning your insides away.

Smiling with pain,
Unhappy til' bled,
Feeding your sins,
With these silent screams.

Screaming with pain,
Yet happy to bleed.

Your blood runs cold
Through your veins,
Screams so loud,
Sounds of suicide.

Pain for happiness,
Bleeding for pleasure.

Smiling with pain,
Unhappy til' bled.
Feeding your sins,
With these silent screams.

Your screams turn to silence
Yet blood is still dripping.

Danielle Worthington (14)
Alderman Smith School, Nuneaton

Seven Ages Poem - Tiger

(Inspired by 'As You Like It' by William Shakespeare)

A tiger's born.
As weak as a fly in a web,
Falling to sleep all the time,
Small and fragile.

A cub.
Eating his mother's prey,
Growing all the time,
Learning to walk.

An energetic cub,
Jumping around like a bouncy ball,
Father teaching him to hunt,
Never getting tired.

A tiger,
Scared of nothing,
Sneaky like a mouse,
Fierce and proud.

A middle-aged tiger
Sleeps all day
Can't be bothered,
But still strong.

An old-aged tiger,
As wobbly as jelly,
Lazy and tired.

A dying tiger,
Can't stand up,
Falls right down,
Dead!

Daniella Deeming (11)
Alderman Smith School, Nuneaton

It's Not My Fault

It's not my fault that he
Fell down the stairs,
He tripped and he fell and
Went over some chairs.

So he said it was me,
But he must be mistaken,
As if I would time
How long it had taken.

To make him fall,
Just for a game?
He has to be wrong,
Or even insane!

I'm his sister, it's wrong
I couldn't do that.
As I said, he fell
And tripped on a mat.

Oops! My story just changed
(and lying was working)
I should plan this more
Carefully and really stop smirking!

As I walk through the door
My brother is there,
He just hugs me and loves me
And fills me with care.

My brother forgave me as
I walked through the door,
But my mother is different
So I fear even more.

Julia Blyth (14)
Alderman Smith School, Nuneaton

The Tentigine

(Based on 'The Wendigo' by Ogden Nash)

The Tentigine
The Tentigine
Gives you shivers down your spine,
Its eyes are bloodshot and angry,
Its blood is fizzy and tangy,
Its mouth is big and gooey,
Slimy,
Smelly,
Its teeth are sharp and large,
And snappy,
Dirty,
Bloody!

The Tentigine
The Tentigine
It is as thick as pine,
It will gobble you up whole,
It sneaks around like it stole,
As you sleep in your bed,
It will bite off your head,
You die,
It is happy,
It sleeps,
Only giving a few peeps.

Kira Sharp (12)
Alderman Smith School, Nuneaton

Parents Poisoning Pears

Parents are not angels,
The way they grunt and groan,
They nag at you for anything,
They like to have their moan.

I bet really they are scheming,
A little plan of theirs.
To turn me into the perfect kid,
By poisoning the pears.

They make me take out the rubbish
And take the dog for a walk,
And when they're watching the TV
I'm not allowed to talk.

While Mum is reading magazines,
And Dad is watching TV,
I'm in the kitchen,
Making cups of tea.

When I do something wrong or bad,
They shout and hiss and rage,
They send me to my bedroom,
As if it is a cage.

Stephanie Johnson (14)
Alderman Smith School, Nuneaton

Football

I think football is really great,
It started way back from a very old date.
Play it at home with your mate,
You'll want to stay out till it's very late!

Play it anywhere, grass, dirt, or path,
'Cause then you'll find out it's a great laugh.
Monday to Sunday, whatever the weather,
Because football will bring the whole world together!

Alex Jones (14)
Alderman Smith School, Nuneaton

Make Poverty History!

No food to eat,
Or water to drink,
These two simple things,
Can make you think.
What is poverty?
What does it do?
None of these things are important to you,
But they are to others,
Who are stuck in this life,
Where they are the ones that pay the price,
Where poverty is taking over their home,
Over the world they have come to know
But we wouldn't understand,
What poverty can do,
Because it doesn't happen,
To me or to you.
Try living their life,
See what they see,
Or simply make poverty history!

Gabriella Robinson (13)
Alderman Smith School, Nuneaton

Chicken Pox

Chicken pox
They come up as sly as a fox.

They are red raw
They are really sore.

They are in every place
On our arms,
All over your face.

John Cooke (14)
Archbishop Grimshaw School, Chelmsley Wood

I Watch, I Saw, I See

I watch how the moon sits in the sky
On my bed while I lie
I watch how the stars twinkle in the light,
So I know it is night.

When the sun shines bright in the morning,
I wake up and start yawning.

The moon's gone in
And the sun's come out
The smell of the fresh grass in the morning
The sun shines on it all
I watch as the trees blow in the wind,
And the river flows by in the green.

When the sun shines bright in the morning,
I wake up and start yawning.

Samantha Perry (14)
Archbishop Grimshaw School, Chelmsley Wood

My Hobby Horse

I have a stunning bay horse
Who I train on the racecourse,
Her name is Juicy,
And my name is Lucy.

Every day I make her train
Even if it's pouring down with rain,
She likes eating apples and sugar
And sometimes she's naughty but I love her.

I plan our day,
As Juicy eats her hay,
When I eat my tea at the table,
My mom goes to feed my horse in her stable!

Brenda Kane (14)
Archbishop Grimshaw School, Chelmsley Wood

Nature

The clear blue sky,
Where the birds happily fly,
Lights up in the day,
And darkens in the night.

The sun shines so bright,
On the hills where I stand,
Where I joyfully fly my kite,
On the clear green land.

The flowers look up to the sun,
As it shines upon them all,
Some flowers are small,
And some are very tall.

The river flows beside the hills,
The clear sparkle of the windmills,
As they spin and collect the wind,
I watch my kite as it blows,
Still the river moves and flows.

Brett Mannion (14)
Archbishop Grimshaw School, Chelmsley Wood

Bully

Bully, bully why hurt me?
Bully, bully, why make me cry?
Do you do this for pleasure,
Don't my standards measure?
I had a friend before you came
Now he's ran away in fear
Since you came along I've been called a queer,
I live in fear
Tell my mom I love her
I'm going to jump
Now how does it feel?
Do you cry now?

Christine O'Reilly (11)
Archbishop Grimshaw School, Chelmsley Wood

Lost Love

You're the one I always wanted
But you never even looked at me.
You ran away from the truth,
And now look where you are.

Waiting for me to hold you
And now look where I am.
Waiting for you to come back to me,
But it's never going to happen.

And now I'm here by your side,
But you're sleeping and I'm thinking,
Should I wake you up? But you say my name
So I say to myself, *'No, I won't.'*

So I leave a rose by your bed
And you will know it was me.
And I'm finally free from my lost love,
So I climb out the window again.

But as I wander the streets,
Your name appears, somehow, always . . .
And as I turn around and look back,
You're following me, watching me.

So I start walking towards you,
And you're running towards me,
I've finally got you and I'm not letting go,
Because I finally found my lost love.

Mark Mulvihill (14)
Archbishop Grimshaw School, Chelmsley Wood

It's OK

Wandering in a field of warmth
Just to fall in a pit of hate,
To see your face, your reflection,
In a cracked mirror.
This pain is just surreal,
And your face haunts my dearest nightmare.
Then you turn around, you watch me drown
Just say something to make it all better.
As I'm all heartbroken, lying all alone,
No light shines in on my heart.
As I disappear, don't pretend to mourn
I wish you would have rescued me from this forgotten fairy tale,
As I'm longing to be free.

I wake up to see you, to feel you, to love you,
As I know you love me and I was only dreaming.
I just want to be with you to see the world how you see it.
It's OK, everything will be alright with you around.
It's been a long, long time without you.
Did you see me when I cried?
I can't stand the thought of being without you,
Or I'll be just where I was before.
And I just want to let you know I love you.

Kimberley Moloney (13)
Archbishop Grimshaw School, Chelmsley Wood

My Cheesy Blink 182 Poem

Travis is covered in tattoos
He dances round in tap shoes.
Tom Delonge has emo hair
In his videos he runs around bare.
Mark Hoppus is a bit of a freak,
He's like that every day of the week.
This is about Blink 182,
Just to say everyone else loves them too.

Terri Evans (14)
Archbishop Grimshaw School, Chelmsley Wood

Her

Praying through the night,
Wishing the stars would fall into the hands of her lover.
He's her life, joy and light,
Never wanting to spend their days without each other.

Every day for them is exciting, passionate and full of romance.
It never could be better.
Like a camouflage Heaven when they dance,
And it seems to last forever.

Dedicating her life and soul to him,
She erases every tear he's ever cried.
He places her hair behind her ear,
All restrictions were denied.

Joined together by a little band of gold,
Three words she whispers into his ear.
A promise to be together until they're older than old.
She no longer sees love as something to fear.

Laura Price (15)
Archbishop Grimshaw School, Chelmsley Wood

Bullied . . .

The time is now drawing near
I slowly fill with fear
As I slowly walk through the gate
I look and see a lot of hate.

He's walking over for my money
This is a time that is not funny
I thought this day could not get worse
I saw myself in a long black hearse.

Bang! He hit me
I want to flee,
Why can't you pick on another kid?
'Cause I can't think of what I did!

Tiffany Chatterley (14)
Archbishop Grimshaw School, Chelmsley Wood

Memories Of You

I count each night that passes by, just pining for the time
When you'll be mine again.
Alone I miss the memory of your kiss,
And dream again of Heaven clutched in your loving arms.
Remembering the times we shared.
I close my eyes to see you there, a living breathing fantasy,
Sighing I think of you sitting beside me, so soft, so smooth,
                                                    so radiant.
Holding me close, stroking my hair, the scent of you haunting me.
A lonely teardrop burns my cheek.
Awake once I sense just emptiness around me.
The rain outside is my mourning friend,
Still longing for the time when you'll be mine again.

Jodie Phillips (14)
Archbishop Grimshaw School, Chelmsley Wood

Untitled

Roses are red, violets are blue,
A face like yours belongs in a zoo
Don't feel bad, don't feel blue,
Frankenstein was ugly too.
On a silent night when friends are few
I close my eyes and think of you,
A silent night, a silent tear,
A silent wish that you was here!
Too many guys want to be like me,
It's starting to get me kind of angry
Take them to the cemetery
Put them six foot deep
Double EP piraters can't test me
When I pull out my gat-ey
It goes *pop, pop, pop, pop*
Roses are red, spiders are black,
Cheat on me and I will break your back!

Jordan Hay (12)
Archbishop Grimshaw School, Chelmsley Wood

Wind-Up Doll

Don't try and ring me,
Don't even call,
Don't try and catch me as I fall,
You weren't there when I needed you most,
I thought you were different,
What a joke,
How wrong was I?
You led me on just like a fool,
But now you must learn the price to pay,
Not that it would matter anyway,
You broke my heart into a thousand shiny pieces,
You shot at me like a dart,
It didn't work, it never will,
You drugged me like some kind of pill,
You never loved me, you never will,
You have just learnt how to kill.
                              Wind-up doll.

Kate Eaton (14)
Archbishop Grimshaw School, Chelmsley Wood

Scully The Bully

There was a man named Scully
He was a really big bully
No way that's funny,
Because for us the day's never sunny.
When we go to school we're running
Just in case he's coming.
When we go to school we hide
Just in case we collide.
Well now you've met Scully
I've really got to go
Why, you say so?
Because the new bully's coming
The *new* bully called Jo!

Thomas Bruce (14)
Archbishop Grimshaw School, Chelmsley Wood

Big Brother

Big Brother, Big Brother,
He's no mother,
Saskia and Maxwell
Under the cover.
Because they are big lovers,
Of each other,
They made the front cover.
Now Saskia's been evicted
Maxwell's still addicted.
Maxwell is sad
And feels so bad.
She's off the hook
In his book.
He needs his girl,
She's a real pearl.
He's a real cockney lad
But misses her like mad.
Davina, Davina, the bearer of bad news,
She's the one who tells them if they win or lose.

Lisa Barrett (13)
Archbishop Grimshaw School, Chelmsley Wood

Bullying

Bullying, bullying, bad or good?
Bullying, bullying, it will give you a thud.
Punch, kick, slap or nut
You have to take the pain when they stamp on your foot.
Black, white, Asian skin
You will have to run or they will put you in the bin.
They will tell you a lie, they will look all sly,
They're coming now,
Goodbye!

Ryan Chapman (12)
Archbishop Grimshaw School, Chelmsley Wood

Athletics

Athletics is good
Athletics is bad
It just depends on the skills that you have

100 metres
The whistle has blown
You pounce off the blocks
Then you zoom, zoom, zoom . . .

400 metres
It's only a lap
You sprint around
Just like that!

1,500 metres
It's hard to run
But it only matters
After the bang of the gun.

Athletics is a solo sport
Rarely working in a team
But to win is my only dream.

Ryan Hewitt (12)
Archbishop Grimshaw School, Chelmsley Wood

Black

Black is a dark colour, it follows you everywhere.
It occurs in the mist and shadows allow you
To think it's not there.
It hides around at daytime and comes out at night,
Which you might not think is scary,
But you'll be in for a fright!

Bruce Shingler (13)
Archbishop Grimshaw School, Chelmsley Wood

The Kingdom

The muscles of power,
A kingdom and crown,
Joyful people,
And a joyful sound.

The song of a tweety bird
Can anyone hear?
The lovely music
To my ear.

Sitting by a fire,
In a rocking chair
As years go by,
So does my hair!

The fame and glory
I once knew
Who should take my place?
Who, who, who?

Aiden Sartin (11)
Archbishop Grimshaw School, Chelmsley Wood

Bullying And Racism

It is nasty and not kind
We should be nice to each other
Bullying, what can I say?
Racism let's keep it away.

This is how to stop bullying
Tell a teacher or the police
Or just anyone
If life becomes too hard to bear.

Sometimes it goes too far
You get beaten up.
It is nasty,
So stop it!

Claire Myatt (12)
Archbishop Grimshaw School, Chelmsley Wood

Poem

When I saw him walking down the street,
Straightaway I took to my feet
When I look up he's just standing there,
All I do is stare and stare.

He's angry and hunts my money
I laugh at him as if it's funny,
All he wants is my cash
Or else he said he'd give me a bash.

I fall to the floor and land on my knees
I beg with him, 'Please, oh please.'
I ask, 'Just don't hurt me!'
'Alright, beat it, flee.'

He's there with a big grin on his face
I walk off and pick up the pace
I get home, slam the door,
And start to cry, falling to the floor.

Daniel Ryan
Archbishop Grimshaw School, Chelmsley Wood

Bully

Bully, bully, why do you hurt me?
Bully, bully, why do you torment me?
Sometimes I bully people, I guess this is just payback,
But now I know what it used to feel like,
To give somebody a kick and a smack.
I know the word that I must say
I just can't bring my heart to say it.
Now I will be bullied for the rest of my life.
I knew as the man pulled out that knife,
I knew that something was going to go
I just didn't realise it was my life.

Nathan Kelly (12)
Archbishop Grimshaw School, Chelmsley Wood

Weather

Weather in the world
Can make you smile
But rain can appear
Once in a while

On a fantasy island
Volcanoes can explode
Molten lava and ash
Lands on the road

In lots of different countries
Storms can begin
Hurricanes and tornadoes
Begin to spin and spin

In other storms thunder bangs
And lightning begins to flash
The blinding light can cause
A horrific and terrible crash

When it snows it's soft and white
But it turns to hail so you must prevail
Because it hurts and
Gives you a fright

The sun comes out but soon goes in
And then some clouds go grey
It's overcast but the clouds won't last
They're sure to go away

The kids come out and shout, 'Hooray!'
They're glad the clouds have gone
The kids run out and run about
So the sun shines on.

Chris Bounds (12) & Mitchell Joy
Archbishop Grimshaw School, Chelmsley Wood

Bullying

Bullying, why?
Is it because you like the sound of a person's cry,
Is it because you're scared,
Because no one at home has ever cared?
Is it because you're just bitter inside?
That you have to make people scared so that when you
Walk down the hall they feel they have to hide?
Is it because you like to be in control,
Is that why you make people want to be swallowed
Up by a big, black hole?
Please tell me your reasons why,
Why you make me want to curl up and die?

Shannon Knight (12)
Archbishop Grimshaw School, Chelmsley Wood

Do Your Best

Even though it hasn't been your day,
And nothing at all is going your way,
Just keep your head up and carry on,
You've still got luck, though you think there's none.
Just try and try to do your best,
If you can make it through half the day, you can make it
Through the rest.
Maybe you'll fail, maybe you'll make it,
But I've got hope, I know you can do it.
If you try you will adore,
Your guardian angel that gives you more,
More hope, more faith, and more space.
Because you can do it, I'll bet that on the human race!
You have family and mates from what I can see
But most of all you have the faith, the faith in me.
Anyone can see that you are really trying,
And that I am not denying.
I'm telling the truth, I'm not lying,
Carry on like this and you will be flying!

Lucy Woodcock (12)
Archbishop Grimshaw School, Chelmsley Wood

Bullying

Why do people pick on others?
Just because they are different,
Just because they don't have any brothers
Do you like to hear people cry,
Or do you just want them to die?
Just because you don't like them
You think you're a gem.
Just because they've got ginger hair,
You think that they care?
Why do you beat them up,
Just because they don't watch the World Cup?
Just because things are bad at home,
You say they don't use a comb!
Why bully, why
Do you make them feel that they want to die?
So say something good,
Don't put their face in the mud!
Just because you think they deserve that,
Don't be a prat!
Say something nice,
And what you get out of it will be twice as much more
Than you normally get,
So think of the happy faces you have met.

Why, why, why?
Don't make them feel like they want to die!

Helen Keane (12)
Archbishop Grimshaw School, Chelmsley Wood

My Poem

Sitting here on the bench,
Thinking of the past
When me and my brother were working in the trench.

Wind blowing, sun shining,
As I placed a poppy down.
Tears streaming down my face,
As I thought of my dear brother Sam.

Sitting here all alone,
No one here to comfort me.
Thinking of me and my brother,
And the times that we have been through.

Victoria Ireland (13)
Archbishop Grimshaw School, Chelmsley Wood

Bullying

Bullying is wrong,
So you've got to be strong,
Then write a song,
And tell me what's wrong.

Don't let bullies drive you mad,
Because in the end you'll end up sad,
You'll cry and cry and they'll be glad,
Which means they are very bad.

Don't let bullies get you down,
'Cause they will win the crown,
They'll laugh and laugh to make you frown,
And then you will feel like a clown.

Tinekka-Jade Pascoe (12)
Archbishop Grimshaw School, Chelmsley Wood

My Last Goodbye

The guns were banging loudly,
People running around madly,
Bullets flying, people dying,
Soldiers fighting proudly.

Bombs falling everywhere,
Enemy soldiers don't care,
They'll shoot you down with no remorse,
Fighting soldiers, a powerful force.

Poverty near, life becoming clear,
Will I die? That's my fear.
I am homeless.
Never to go home again:
For my home went up in flames.

Memories lost, never to be found,
My family lay a poppy down,
As my dead body lay in the ground.

Maisie Parry (14)
Archbishop Grimshaw School, Chelmsley Wood

War

When I look around all I see is war
Whether it's another country or on ya front door
'Cause people are arguing more and more
Everyone's fighting, the rich and the poor.

People getting killed in the sky,
Getting jumped or shot in a drive-by
Making people's mammas cry
For the fun of killing any common guy!

James Jones-Styzaker (14)
Archbishop Grimshaw School, Chelmsley Wood

Bullying

Bullying is bad,
People who get bullied are sad
They go crying, to their mom
But the bullies think it's fun.

They bully them outside school
They bully them inside school
The bullies think they rule
But they are jerks after all.

The teachers try to help them
It turns to the bully that gets them
They hit and punch
And they bully them in a bunch.

The headmaster is trying to do the best
But the bullies do all the rest
They find them and tell them
If they tell they will get them.

In the end of it all
The bullies don't rule no more.

Perry Nash (12)
Archbishop Grimshaw School, Chelmsley Wood

War

Many families torn apart
But the thought never reaches his heart
Just eighteen and holds a gun
Does he wonder what he's done?
All of this over oil,
Blood of men in the soil,
Suffering suicide, homeless too,
All this pain just for you,
Or . . . so he says.

Sarah Grice (14)
Archbishop Grimshaw School, Chelmsley Wood

Bullying!

Why oh why do you bully me?
Is it jealousy or is it just me?
It's so wrong, oh can't you see?
So why oh why do you bully me?

I went home bleeding yesterday,
I told my mom it was OK
When I told my dad he went astray,
So think about it now, OK
Why do you hate me anyway?

I was crying and got stabbed two days ago
I tried to fit in and go with the flow
After that you told me to go, I said no,
You pulled out a knife and said, 'Well, let's go!'

Kyle Fennell (12)
Archbishop Grimshaw School, Chelmsley Wood

Bullying

Bullying is no fun
Building my life isn't that easy
I just start crying, then I get wheezy
People are sad,
Why are bullies bad?

You hurt people's feelings,
What about the meanings?
Oi, oi, bully, why are you there?
Are you waiting for a victim over there?

Natasha Dickenson (12)
Archbishop Grimshaw School, Chelmsley Wood

Still Remains

Lay a poppy down to die,
Forget me not but please, don't cry.
I did all I ever wanted to
My only regret is losing you.

I fought for my country, stood up proud
Bombs fall crashing down, so loud.
Blood splattered where houses lay,
Fire burnt it all away.

Rain washed away the pain,
But the heartache still remains,
From now until forever dies,
Will still remain my last goodbyes.

Dannielle Brickley (14)
Archbishop Grimshaw School, Chelmsley Wood

Racism

Black or white,
Blue or green,
Small or big,
We're all the same
Human beings
Fat or slim
Loud or not
Rich or poor,
It doesn't matter
We're all the same
We're all the same
It's just the colour,
But we're still all human beings.

    We're all the same!

Kellie Light & Kirsty Jackson (12)
Archbishop Grimshaw School, Chelmsley Wood

London Bombing

With people bombing what is the world coming to?
People screaming, people dying,
London bombing, going off.
People scared to walk the street.
Family members getting worried.
Will they see their family again?

Bombing other places, what is the world coming to?
Young children without mummies or daddies.
Different family members left to bring them up . . .

Danielle Billingsley (13)
Archbishop Grimshaw School, Chelmsley Wood

Anti-Racism

Doesn't matter colour of skin,
Racism is a deadly sin,
White and black, black and white,
We must not start a lifetime fight.

Different if everyone could not see
Racism would not be
So everyone should lose their sight,
Black and white should unite.

Joel Mallabar (12)
Archbishop Grimshaw School, Chelmsley Wood

Happiness

Happiness makes you think of a smile
Your blood flows around like the River Nile,
Your heart is so strong
You burst into song
I didn't know happiness could last so long.

Amy Masters (13)
Archbishop Grimshaw School, Chelmsley Wood

Bullying

B ullying, well what can I say?
U put up with it until one day
L ife becomes too hard to bear
L imping, bruised, no one to care.
'Y oung boy on the wall
I say, boy with the ball.
N o one to hang around with
G oing out on your own?'

Ryan Muldowney (12)
Archbishop Grimshaw School, Chelmsley Wood

Dulce Et Decorum Est

(Inspired by 'Dulce et Decorum est' by Wilfred Owen)

D ying in trenches
U nder ceaseless fire
L iving with rats
C an this war be hatred?
E ven if we have to die.

E ndure the sunshine
T hey endure death.

D eath is the answer
E ven to them as well
C olour isn't important, land is
O ther than that
R omania will pay
U nder my pillow holds a
M achine gun for a surprise attack.

E ventually they
S urrender with a white flag
T urrets shoot at the enemy.

Jamie Hewitt (12)
Ash Green School, Ash Green

Heartache

The rain is raining hard outside
Droplets leak onto my page
But they are not droplets from the heavy rainfall
But tears from my heart.

The blistering heat shines a beam of light
Onto my face
But these tears will never dry
And my heart will never heal.

As it turns night, the stars come out
They twinkle and glisten but it's
Painful to watch.
Because it reminds me of his eyes
When he looked at me.

As the trees sway in the wind
And the grass blows in the breeze,
It seems like I can no longer
Keep my eyes open
Because it reminds me of his dear face.

The rhythm of the birds reminds me
Of the same beat in my heart
When he looked at me
Because I know for a second
I crossed his mind.

This love is a heartache.

Selina Chauhan (14)
Ash Green School, Ash Green

My Favourite Two Seasons

Winter! What a cold time of year,
The trees asleep, branches blowing in the wind
Only a few birds around with no song to sing,
The ground to hand and animals struggle
They burrow deep down to keep warm and snuggle.
People hurry from home to car, to travel near or travel far
Winter is a lonely time with pavements dirty and full of grime.

Spring is an exciting time of year,
Small bulbs emerging through the soil after
Their long winter's toil to grow and bloom.
The trees awaken with small buds of growth
They spread along the branches like a cloak.
Daffodils and tulips shoot up towards the sky,
As the sun warms our planet a few will die.
The birds return with a song to sing,
A peaceful time carried on the brisk wind.

Lewis Jones (12)
Ash Green School, Ash Green

The Dark Journey Home

It was growing dark
The wind wanted to tell you a secret
But an owl hoots,
Something is lying in your path
Is it a monster, or just a tree?
Quick, run and jump, you made it, well done!
The moon lights your way
Rotten hands grab at you or are they just twigs?
Quick, the howlings are creeping closer.
You see a light on and open the gate
Start knocking on the door.
Just to find nobody's home . . .

Courtney Hastie
Ash Green School, Ash Green

Dulce Et Decorum Est

(Inspired by 'Dulce et Decorum est' by Wilfred Owen)

D ying in trenches
U nder ceaseless fire
L iving with rats
C alling out for help
E ver wanting to be free

E ggs, tea and cheese
T ill our dying day

D eath's here, death's there
E very day grows harder
C oughing all day, all night
O ver hills, through tunnels
R unning here and there
U nexplainable pain
M achine guns left on the floor

E ver thinking, why such a war?
S moke covers the sky
T onight they rest, tomorrow they fight.

Paige Barratt (12)
Ash Green School, Ash Green

Dulce Et Decorum Est

(Inspired by 'Dulce et Decorum est' by Wilfred Owen)

D ying in trenches
U nder ceaseless fire
L iving with rats
C ountless miles of gunshells
E ven bodies are scattered around

E veryone just fight, fight, fight!
T o the point, where no one lives

D ecorated are the fields
E ven colours of brown and red
C olours of hate and distress
O pen the hands of peace should be
R eady to accept other countries
U nderneath are the colours of peace
M aybe they're not that easy to see

E veryone unite
S top war now
T his is your warning.

Hollie Docker (12)
Ash Green School, Ash Green

Dulce Et Decorum Est

(Inspired by 'Dulce et Decorum est' by Wilfred Owen)

D ying in trenches
U nder ceaseless fire
L iving with rats
C ans were all we could
E at from

E ating was our main thought
T he food was disappearing like clouds

D eadly fighting day and night
E xplosions were never-ending
C louds of smoke made it hard to breathe
O vernight we try to rest
R unning around early in the morning
U nderneath us the ground is full of mines
M y mind's never at rest

E ach day seems to last a year
S ometimes I wish it would all be over
T hen we could all go back to our families.

Lewis Morris (12)
Ash Green School, Ash Green

Dulce Et Decorum Est

(Inspired by 'Dulce et Decorum est' by Wilfred Owen)

D ying in trenches
U nder ceaseless fire
L iving with rats
C rying soldiers in pain
E verywhere anger

E verywhere there's pain
T housands of bombs and bullets

D ying people struggling to live
E ndless fear of death
C annons constantly firing
O fficers commanding
R unning soldiers
U nthinkable smells of burning flesh
M adness everywhere

E very person smells the fire
S ees the death
T ouches the dead.

Beth Calcott (12)
Ash Green School, Ash Green

Dulce Et Decorum Est

(Inspired by 'Dulce et Decorum est' by Wilfred Owen)

D ying in trenches
U nder ceaseless fire
L iving with rats
C annons fire at shore
E veryone races to fight

E veryone torn apart as they run
T ons of ammo laid to waste

D ead bodies lie to waste across the beach
E ach one dead
C annons fade away
O ver the shore the Germans run
R ed sea for miles around
U nder no fire the screams fall
M urdered men stripped for ammo

E veryone boards the ship
S ilence falls as the Germans retreat
T he day brightens as the ship goes.

Steven Davies (12)
Ash Green School, Ash Green

The Nasgul

In a wood not far from here,
There lives a creature of many names,
And if you look into its eyes
Your soul will burn in flames.

Its teeth as sharp as daggers
Its eyes like blood-red pools
Its breath is hot as lava red
And its name is the Nasgul.

And in this forest dark
One thousand bodies lie
And they're all dead because
They heard the Nasgul's cry.

Beneath its bulky belly
Lies a glittering hoard,
Diamond, ruby and sapphires blue
And the golden hilt of a sword.

Its angry roar, like thunder
It's bigger than a house
But the only thing to scare this beast
Is a tiny chocolate mouse!

Andrew Walker (12)
Ash Green School, Ash Green

Me And You!

I remember that day,
That party,
I gave you a hug,
You gave me one back,
You gave me that look,
I gave you it back.
You held my hand,
And of course I held it back.
You said you liked me,
I told you that too.
I wish I never,
Because now look at us two.
Can't we go back, to how we were?
Just two good friends,
Because it's becoming a blur.

Stevie Roberts (13)
Ash Green School, Ash Green

Friendship

Sometimes we laugh
Sometimes we cry
But this does not matter
Because our friendship will never die.

I will always be there for you
No matter what happens
I will always care for you.

When you are down
I will lift your head high
So you are not staring at the ground
But staring at the sky.

I am so proud that you are my friend
This is something I will never pretend
I will always be your best friend.

Rosie Wood (11)
Ash Green School, Ash Green

Summer

Butterflies flutter from
Leaf to leaf,
Birds fly in the air,
From tree to tree,
Bumblebees hover,
Flower to flower
Slugs munch at the leaves
Crunch, crunch
Ducks swim in the lake
Paddle, paddle
Fish blow bubbles in the water
Gurgle, gurgle
Vegetables, flowers, shrubs, herbs
Grow out of the ground,
Runner beans shoot,
Out of the ground,
Daisies pop through the grass,
Weak shrubs peeping out of the earth,
People mow the grass,
Becoming hot and frustrated,
People trim the lawns,
Men cut the hedge,
Buzz, buzz,
Women picking the crops
Getting hot,
Hot sun sizzling,
Sun beaming down.

James Townsley
Ash Green School, Ash Green

Dolphins

Dolphins are the very best
Better than all the rest,
Playing games all day long
Singing to a happy song.

Splashing in the deep blue sea
Can't wait to be near you and me,
Wouldn't hurt a single fly
Waving to fish as they pass by.

Dolphins are so very clever
Thick as a brick, they were never,
Dancing and twirling to the beat
Watch the way they move their feet.

Dolphins are really cool
Performing shows in a pool
Doing all the fancy tricks
Jumping over very high sticks.

Dolphins are the very best
Better than all the rest
Playing games all day long
Singing to a happy song.

Shannon Kincade (11)
Ash Green School, Ash Green

The Magic Box

(Based on 'Magic Box' by Kit Wright)

I will put in my box
A sound of a spooky ghost
A taste of a vampire's blood
A noise of a witch laughing.

I will put in my box
A touch of a silky sari,
A smell of a diva lightning
A bang of a colourful firework.

I will put in my box
A smell of a Christmas pudding,
A taste of a salad,
A crack of a cracker.

The twinkling star like a banana
The sound of a referee whistling
The taste of a pumpkin.

My box is fully coloured
With yellow sparkling sand,
The colour of a beach waving
And lots of people cheering.

Namrata Bhardwaj (11)
Ash Green School, Ash Green

The Nightmare

Banging and crashing throughout the night,
Nightmares are about to give you a fright,
Mummies digging to get out of their graves,
Dracula's laughing and calling your name,
Thunder and lightning winds howling aloud,
Saying, 'We're coming to get you, it's not in your head!'
Ghouls and ghosts are haunting your home
They're in the shadows,
Get out! Get out!
They may whisper in your ear,
They may play with your hair,
They might throw things around,
Or just stand and stare.
The sun is about to rise
Everyone starts to wake
Mum shouts, 'Breakfast's ready!'
Thank God I'm alive and last night has passed.
I didn't think the night would ever end.
That was one nightmare I don't want again!

Paula Sears (12)
Ash Green School, Ash Green

My Cat

I have a little cat,
He looks a sad little chap,
His fur is all a mess,
But I love him nonetheless.

He brightens up my day,
Every time we play,
He is only very small,
He curls up in a ball.

He has very furry feet,
And likes his can of meat,
He likes his drop of milk,
His fur feels like silk.

His name is Scruff,
His tongue is rough,
He has a little bed,
Where he curls up after he has been fed!

Chelsee-Jade Hollihead (12)
Ash Green School, Ash Green

Bigger Than Our World

The grasp of a hand holding the world in a net,
Makes our world seem as small as an insect
Our world cupped into a net,
The colourful background makes the scene feel happy and cheerful
But unrealistic
A man's hand, bigger than our world.

Abigail Spencer (13)
Bigwood Secondary School, Warren Hill

Picnic In The Thunder

Family day out
Loud annoying noise
Healthy green grass
Terrifying
Birds singing
Using light in an evil way.

Radiant sun
The sky darkens as black as coal
Gentle calm wind
Waiting for the class to arrive
Long tall trees to give us shade
The loudness seems to sound like an angry mole.

Red and white checked blanket
The fear is like a cold chill down your spine
Variety of different food . . . *mmm*
Every day we pray it to be a day late
Lots of laughing
Sometimes they come true
Having fun
Sometimes they don't.

Onome Abara (13)
Bigwood Secondary School, Warren Hill

Thunder At The Picnic

Loud, crashing sandwiches,
Warm bolts flash around.
Noisy bees enjoy the sun
Bellowing geese chase us
Frightening grass sways in the wind
House-shaking teddy bears.

Kristie Butler (13)
Bigwood Secondary School, Warren Hill

Rain

Down comes the rain
The river is flowing
Down in Spain
The man is moving

Plip plop plip plop
Down comes the rain
Plip plop plip plop
It's driving me insane

Down comes the rain
In the river there's fish
Being attacked by a crane
The fish is on a dish

Plip plop plip plop
Down comes the rain
Plip plop plip plop
It's driving me insane

Down comes the rain
And the lightning too
It's landing on the plane
The plane is blue

Plip plop plip plop
Down comes the rain
Plip plop plip plop
It's driving me insane.

Lee Sykes (13)
Bigwood Secondary School, Warren Hill

My Poem

Sitting in this window looking out on my world
Crying in this window longing for something else
Dreaming in this window of what could've been
Knowing that one day you were my world.

What should I do to end the pain?
Will I ever feel love again?
It's harder than you think to forget about you
Maybe that's why I'm feeling so blue.

Although now what's done is done
It's over, finished we've had our fun
You broke my heart and made it shatter
But I guess to you that doesn't matter.

Romy Idle (13)
Bigwood Secondary School, Warren Hill

My Thundery Picnic Poem

The loud but peaceful atmosphere,
The scary food blanket

The noisy grass
The gloomy trees

And the boring shorts and skirts.

The dark adventurous birds,
The sad and sunny sun hats,

The bright but polite flowers,
Colourful laughter of the kids,

And the growling of the lion's mane.

Terri Charles (13)
Bigwood Secondary School, Warren Hill

I See You!

There is an oval pocket in your head,
Holding a great ball which sees all!

The forest of hair around the oval pocket,
Flutters in places.
The glass ball which comes
In multiple colours can sometimes leak!
It might need help,
Like glasses, they will help!
I am an eye!
I can see you who else

Oh yeah you're reading this!

You too

And you

You too

And especially you,
So watch out!

Ashley Warsop (13)
Bigwood Secondary School, Warren Hill

The Rose

You water it with a hose
You smell it with your nose
This flower is called a rose
The rose will eventually pose
The rose will tickle your toes
When it dies you have many woes.
The rose.

Maciey Freestone-McDonald (13)
Bigwood Secondary School, Warren Hill

The Neon Street

He started walking,
Down the street,
Neon signs glowing,
Dancing to the beat.

The rain was beating on his hat,
And on his long brown coat,
Reaching into the puddles on the floor,
As if it was a boat.

Unbeknownst to him,
Somebody followed,
Stalking with a pistol,
Because he owed.

Taking his girlfriend,
Was my biggest mistake,
Now I have drowned,
At the bottom of a lake.

Peter Revill (12)
Bigwood Secondary School, Warren Hill

Babi-Blue-Licous

Are we looking for Heaven?
It's as blue as can be
It's nothing like that Devon
It's pretty as I can see.

It's a dream come true
A land of imagination.

Are we angels?
Are we devils?
Or are we humans?

Who owns this beautiful sight?

Lauren Chambers (13)
Bigwood Secondary School, Warren Hill

My Ballad

She sneaked up to the door,
The shadow was of a man crying,
The light shine upon the floor,
He strolled up to the door sighing.

She leaned on the door,
It fell open with a bang,
She fell over onto the floor,
Then she smiled as he sang.

He then asked, 'Do you like me Leah?'
Her response was, 'No you're queer!'
He chucked her on the floor,
She slammed against the swinging door.

Sophie Barker (13)
Bigwood Secondary School, Warren Hill

War Way

The last gunshot was fired,
Everywhere was silent,
The war-wounded soldiers were tired,
Even though the war was won,
There were no smiles on their faces,
Because the damage was already done.

The sun was setting fast,
But the soldiers were slow,
The war had seemed to last forever,
The soldiers couldn't wait to see their loved ones,
But there was a long journey home,
Although many soldiers had gone.

Penny Waltham (13)
Bigwood Secondary School, Warren Hill

My Poem!

The storms disturbed us,
The weather was confused,
The skies were a deep, dark red,
It wasn't natural.

The lightning cracked,
Electricity, the sky did not lack,
As the lightning struck,
My bedroom lit up.

As the thunder boomed,
The darkness loomed,
It made me jump,
I hate the sound.

As darkness fell,
Nothing I could feel,
But cold,
And insecurity.

Lucy Williams (12)
Bigwood Secondary School, Warren Hill

I See

I look into your eyes,
And what I see,
Are deep pools of green
And the reflections of me.

I see the sun shining bright
And the stars in the sky.
I see people dancing
And birds flying by.

Niamh Hickey (13)
Bigwood Secondary School, Warren Hill

Life Goes On . . .

Days go by, and life goes on
I wish you could be here,
I toss and turn when I go to sleep
I can't believe that you aren't here.

You kissed my cheek
You held my hand, all your love is my demand
Now the summer's come and gone,
I miss you babe, it's been so long.

I smell your musky scent where you lay beside me
On that night that brought your death,
And you said you'd stand by me.

When the winter goes again the chill will always be here
And when I finally pass to be with you,
We will be together again dear.

Melissa Blake (13)
Bigwood Secondary School, Warren Hill

She Didn't Know

She didn't know
That I was there,
She didn't know
I stopped and stared.

She didn't know
What I knew
She didn't know
Her life would be through
She didn't know
I would attack,
She didn't know
She had a knife in her back!

Jennie Wallace (13)
Bigwood Secondary School, Warren Hill

Love

(Dedicated to Mark Stredder)

Love is red
Love is pink
Love can happen within a blink.

It makes your heart yell
It makes your heart skip a beat
It makes you not want to eat.

You become flimsy
You become shaken
Your heart has been taken.

Not a word is said
Not a word is spoken
Not knowing your heart may be
Broken.

Love!

Rochelle Freestone-McDonald (13)
Bigwood Secondary School, Warren Hill

The Rock

Floating through the air
As hot as the deep burning sun.

A giant rock hurtling towards nothing.

Crash!

Burning through the galaxy
Like volcano lava
Burning through a town.

Hurtling through the galaxy
As fast as 10,000 Ferraris!

Wain Marriott (13)
Bigwood Secondary School, Warren Hill

Poem

There's too many bands,
That jump and shout.

The bands are sometimes in the newspaper
Because they've done something wrong.

Bands like The Darkness
And pop stars jump around too much.

These days bands go on holiday to get away
From the paparazzi.

The paparazzi take juicy photos of pop stars
Taking their girlfriends or wives on holiday.

The bands are sometimes bad or good
When they are on stage.

Bands make you laugh and cry.

They can also raise money for things like Live 8
To save people's lives and people that only have
Three minutes to live.

Jenna Shipman (14)
Bigwood Secondary School, Warren Hill

It Came Back

As the year came back, the year I feared most,
I hoped and prayed, prayed that it wouldn't take
Another part of me
Like it did a year ago.
It has come back to do the same again
The thing that everyone fears the most
The word that no one likes to mention
The word,
        Cancer.

Charlotte Haywood (13)
Bigwood Secondary School, Warren Hill

The Rose

It burst into life in a matter of seconds
Just to die and wilt away
By Mother Nature it was beckoned
To bring me joy every day.

Its beautiful petals shone in the sun
Red as a woman's lips
An amazing flower it had become
The colour darkened at the tip.

Leaving a heavenly streak
The rose eventually died away
As it was too frail and weak
The rose dropped down in a day.

The bush is left without its flower
Into the darkness it will go
From the light and heat it will cower
Swaying to and fro.

The leaves will shrivel and become brown
To leave its visitors with a frown
The rose had come and the rose did go
But in the heart of the bush a new one will grow
It will glow and it will shine
Bringing joy to this heart of mine
Growing strong, growing tall
This time it will not fall
It will stay, never go
What will happen, we will never know . . .

Ashley Shepherd (13)
Bigwood Secondary School, Warren Hill

Everybody's Dream

A beach,
A beach so calm, relaxing and bright
Many people sigh because of the sight
It's everybody's dream.

A ground so dry that it bites your feet
The blue calm sea drifts out and then in.
This all happens to a beat
It's everybody's dream.

No clouds in the sky,
No sight of rain,
A place to relax, not driving you insane.
The children are in the sea, or playing in the sand.
All you want now is to be fanned!
It's everybody's dream.

Katie McEvoy (13)
Bigwood Secondary School, Warren Hill

A Garden Full Of Nature

A garden full of nature,
Plants, flowers and trees
It's like a forest of heaven
The leaves are as green as can be.

This garden is as beautiful as a mountain top,
This garden is nowhere near a filthy shop.
Green, great and glittering,
Light, wonderful and colourful,
A garden full of nature.

Sean Duryea (13)
Bigwood Secondary School, Warren Hill

The Phoenix

It is majestical and proud,
Rises from the ashes
Burns whatever it pleases,
Impossible to kill,
Can get ill,
Can fly wherever it wants
Has strong powers
A great bird of fire
It never gives up
Fire-red eyes,
Fire-red body to match
And a razor-sharp beak.

Mark Thornton (13)
Bigwood Secondary School, Warren Hill

Family

F amily are the ones near to your heart
A lways there in times good or bad
M um gives you kisses, cuddles too
 I n spite of everything they still love you
L et them know how much you care
Y our family is always there.

Rebecca Sabin (13)
Bigwood Secondary School, Warren Hill

The Snake

A snake moves like a worm wriggling above the soil.
Their skin is as smooth as a polished bar table.
The snake's tongue is like a fork in the road.
It coils up like a rope then attacks like a spring.

Nathan Judge (13)
Bigwood Secondary School, Warren Hill

Loneliness

An empty shadow is following my every move
A cage of nothingness and darkness trapping me inside my mind.
No way to retreat.

No light in this darkness
No ray of hope that someday I will be free
A never-ending nothingness that has wrapped itself around me.

A dark void that I have fallen into.
I can feel nothing but the feeling of falling deeper and faster
Into darkness.
Into nothingness
Into . . .
Loneliness.

Rebecca Armes (13)
Bigwood Secondary School, Warren Hill

Love

Love is a sweet thing to say
Because people are there for you every step of the way
And they are on your side when people are nasty to you.
In sickness and in health and till death passes.

Shannen Naylor (13)
Bigwood Secondary School, Warren Hill

Friends

Friends help you when you're feeling down.
Friends are there when no one's around.
Friends help you through thick and thin.
Friends are people who care for you.
Friends, that's what they do.

Jamie McGougan (13)
Bigwood Secondary School, Warren Hill

The Seaside

A hot, sunny day with trees flowing in the breeze,
A relaxing, sandy heaven,
I see footprints in the sand,
With boats sailing away in the distance,
Small creatures swept away by the sea.

The beach is deserted,
A mysterious, lost palace of sand and sea,
The seaside is the only place to be!

Adam Robinson (13)
Bigwood Secondary School, Warren Hill

Darkness

It's lurking in the darkness
It's in your mind,
Look around you, heads hidden in Hell.
They smell of vermin, they're swirling
Round and round in your head.
You look around you're in a room
Full of death
Monsters trying to get you
It's coming . . . death!

Luke Butler (13)
Bigwood Secondary School, Warren Hill

The Night

Interesting patches of red, black and green
Darkness hits the sky as the night draws in
The leaves at the bottom of the picture look like hands,
The scene looks sad and lifeless,
Houses so carefully placed under the orange night's sky.

Jodie Sturman (13)
Bigwood Secondary School, Warren Hill

The Seaside Shore

It's a place with little specks on a gentle and settled sea.
With the sky so blue and clouds so white,
Waiting for the hot summer's light.
Beyond the light there's a crowd so bright
Look behind to the grass so green
Shone by light it makes it look so bright.
People then say goodnight to the sky
That turns to night.

Samantha Swinscoe (13)
Bigwood Secondary School, Warren Hill

The Mysterious Fellow

He is as tall as a ladder,
His hair is like the bright sun,
He bangs on this door,
It goes bang, bing, hong, swing, swong,
His eyes are like the bright blue sky,
His sunglasses are jet-black
He has red fire lips
He has steel muscles.

Luke Waine (13)
Bigwood Secondary School, Warren Hill

Untitled

High on the mountain,
Overlooking the valley,
Snow fills the hollows,
Cold and icy peaks,
The sky overhead,
Red, yellow, orange,
Different shades of blue.
The snow, a lilac tone.

Ashley Whitehead (13)
Bigwood Secondary School, Warren Hill

This Morning

I wake up this morning at 7 o'clock
I sit on my bed and nod off
The alarm goes off at 8 o'clock
I hear on the door: *knock, knock, knock!*

I jump out of bed
I bang my head
I fall on the floor
And think I'm dead.

I'm going to be late
I will miss the gate
I'll get a DT
Mum will shout at me!

I need to eat
Or I'll feel really weak
Give me some food
Or I'll get in a mood.

I'm ready, let's go
Ow, I just bumped my toe
I'm off to school
See ya later bro!

Heather Auckland (12)
Caludon Castle Business and Enterprise Specialist School, Wyken

Summer!

Sunbathers scorch in the shining sun
The shivering sea shakes
Butterflies beautifully beam
Gentle breeze and refreshing rain
The sizzling of the sun
It doesn't seem to matter
Everybody has fun!

Beth Cain (11)
Caludon Castle Business and Enterprise Specialist School, Wyken

The Life Of A Car Tuner

T uning for life
H & R for the superb sound and style
E tech for the unique styling

L owering the car
I ce the competing car
F inish the project and be proud
E ibach for the perfect suspension

O wning the best tuned car is the dream
F or every car tuner in the world

A dmiring the finished product

C hrome wheels making it *bling-bling*
A cting from the heart, the eye and the mind
R aising money by racing

T uning the power and adrenaline by tuning the performance
U ptaking the most difficult challenges of car tuning
N OS for extra bursts of speed
E vos are the best
R acing and cruising. *Vroom!*

Diviyen Mistry (12)
Caludon Castle Business and Enterprise Specialist School, Wyken

Before I Go To Bed Tonight

Before I go to bed tonight
I think of you fondly it's true,
You'll never leave my thoughts,
All night,
Sitting in my room,
Wishing you were here,
Loving you always,
Isn't any of this clear?
Before I go to bed tonight.

Siân Lucas (13)
Caludon Castle Business and Enterprise Specialist School, Wyken

Ice Cream!

Ice cream is great
I could eat eight
I could eat it all day
No one should ever take it away

Ice cream comes in different shapes and sizes
Ice cream is great for weddings and parties
Vanilla, orange, lemon and choc chip
It puts all the weight onto your hip.

Parents say that this is bad for you
But we all know this isn't true!
Now I am gonna get some more
And grab my money and run out the door!

Lauren McDonell (12)
Caludon Castle Business and Enterprise Specialist School, Wyken

The Maze

In leafy green hedges, the doorway was wide,
You look and you wonder and then step inside
The puzzling pathways take you along,
A turn to the left, turned out to be wrong.
A turn to the left, a turn to the right,
You enter the centre, a wonderful sight.
But now comes the hard part,
To find the right track,
To retrace your steps, the secret path back.
The maze is a trickster, of that there's no doubt,
The maze lets you in,
But will it let you out . . . ?

Lewis O'Brien (13)
Caludon Castle Business and Enterprise Specialist School, Wyken

Galloping

Galloping, galloping through the snow
Galloping, galloping here we go
Galloping here
Galloping there
Galloping, galloping everywhere!
Through the wind, the rain, the snow,
Galloping, galloping we must go,
Galloping home,
Galloping back,
Clippety-cloppety,
Hooves on the track.

Charley-Rose Borgeat (12)
Caludon Castle Business and Enterprise Specialist School, Wyken

The Hunter

The hunter, the hunter
In the dark, gloomy forest,
The hunter, the hunter,
Hunting for its prey.

The hunter sees a shadow
The shadow of a deer,
The sound of a gunshot
Then the forest goes dead

The hunter, the hunter
In the dark, gloomy forest
The hunter, the hunter
Hunting for its prey.

The forest without deer
Is like a river with no fish.

Bethany McKenna (12)
Caludon Castle Business and Enterprise Specialist School, Wyken

The Weather

The weather changes day to day
Sunshine, cloudy, rain,
When it's sunny, children play
It really is a pain.

The weather changes every day.

One minute bright, the next it's grey
When the sun shines down, it's cosy and warm.
When the big black clouds come producing a storm.

Next comes the rain, wet and cold,
Making you feel sad, fed-up and old.
Here comes the bang and the lightning from the sky,
Running through the field, you hope it stays high.

Sophie Stuart (13)
Caludon Castle Business and Enterprise Specialist School, Wyken

The Monster

We stopped to see a big black thing,
A monster with claws as sharp as knives,
And skin as black as the night,
I stood beside him and saw his height,
His eyes were as round as balls,
And it made sounds as loud as a bang,
And it had very sharp fangs.
It thumped and crashed across the ground,
And trampled all over the mounds.
His teeth were as sharp as his claws,
And he bit through all of the floors.
It acted like a big bulldozer
As it wrecked and tattered the land,
It grabbed me and tore me apart,
Like a predator tears his prey.

Liam Mistry (11)
Caludon Castle Business and Enterprise Specialist School, Wyken

Animals

Animals, animals everywhere
Growling and barking without a care.
They run through fields at the speed of light
If people get in their way, they give them a bite.

Others are cute and cuddly though
Their eyes shine like a diamond's glow.
Young puppies and kittens play all night
But sometimes they have a little fight.
They chase their tails and roll everywhere,
Get dirt and mud all over the ground.
After all, they get very tired
Then fall asleep in front of the fire.

Jade Horgan (13)
Caludon Castle Business and Enterprise Specialist School, Wyken

My Birthday

It's my birthday
I will be eight
It's my birthday,
I'm having a cake.

It's my birthday,
I'm having a party,
It's my birthday
I've learnt karate.

It's my birthday,
I got lots of toys,
It's my birthday,
I kissed the boys.

It's my birthday,
Today, today,
It's my birthday,
Hooray . . . hooray!

Laura Wedgbury (12)
Caludon Castle Business and Enterprise Specialist School, Wyken

Summer

Summer strolls on
It tiptoes through the dark, cold cities
As calm as usual as it gently floats
Like a feather across the sky.

Summer's here,
Blazing hot!
Time for a holiday!
Children shouting, ice creams melting,
Both sky and sun as bright
And cheerful as children
In the smooth, cold water.

Birds tweeting, children singing
Like a beauty on their cheeks
Trees whistling with the wind
Children hopping like kangaroos.

Summer's gone, no more sun
Autumn has taken over
It's back to short days
And dark nights.

Stanley Saungweme (12)
Caludon Castle Business and Enterprise Specialist School, Wyken

My Monster

Its teeth were as sharp as spikes, just waiting to eat its prey,
Its eyes were red like burning fire, destroying lives on its way,
It moves as fast as a cheetah sprinting to pounce on anything it sees,
He sounds angry like a bear starving,
His body is as strong as a dinosaur, roaring, *rah! Rah! Rah!*
Its claws are as sharp as a sword slicing its enemy.

Navraj Chahal (11)
Caludon Castle Business and Enterprise Specialist School, Wyken

Summer

Summer slithered like a snake silently into season
The shivering ice slowly melted revealing the liveliness inside.

Rushing, rushing, getting hot
Money going from my money pot
The ice cream man getting rich
Sweaty, sweaty, itch, itch, itch.

Days getting shorter
Crawling away
Day by day
Now it's winter once again
Heating turned on
The summer screaming
Fading away.

Leigh Bell
Caludon Castle Business and Enterprise Specialist School, Wyken

The Summer Poem!

The sun beams gracefully on the shivering sea
My mum's roasting in the sun just like me
The clouds float high in the fluffy sky
I hear the chirping birds fly by.

Chloe Evatt (12)
Caludon Castle Business and Enterprise Specialist School, Wyken

Summer

The heat thumped me
My clothes were hugging me
The ice-cold wind ran towards me
The heat fried me to a crisp.

Iknam Chaven (11)
Caludon Castle Business and Enterprise Specialist School, Wyken

Football

Football
As the crowd shouts
Goal!
As the crowd erupts even louder
Boo!
The referee shows a red card
Walking off in shame
As the sun glows on
The shiny pitch.

Steven Cotton (11) & Arranvir Dosanjh (12)
Caludon Castle Business and Enterprise Specialist School, Wyken

Autumn

A ll day long leaves are falling
U nicorns awake when the sun starts dawning
T rees start dying as leaves fall
U nicorn babies try to crawl
M other unicorns make sure they don't slip
N ow the baby ones can run and skip.

Perri McMahon (12)
Caludon Castle Business and Enterprise Specialist School, Wyken

A Death's Tale

You lie on your final bed,
Thinking of what awaits,
You can only dread
Taking that final breath.
Only then will you embrace death,
A coldness crawling through your mind,
A life flashes of what you've left behind
Only then will your eyes begin to close
And your final breath will pass your nose.

Dominic Dutton (13)
Churnet View Middle School, Leek

Three Wishes

If three wishes I had, what would they be?
To see a big monkey in a tree?
No, free the world from poverty.
My second wish would be something mildly good . . . at least
Wake up the dead, the deceased.
That wouldn't work so how about world peace?
Now my third wish, I can only think of one thing . . .
For the world to be without lies and deceit.

Lisa Marie Payne (13)
Churnet View Middle School, Leek

The Lion

The lion sees his prey and licks his lips at the sight.
His lissom lithe body leaps over the ground
His long, lean legs stretch out
And he catches his prey.
Lazily, he lies down,
Spreading out after the lovely meal.

Holly Bailey (13)
Churnet View Middle School, Leek

Summer

Summer is like the colour yellow
Bright and cheerful
Summer makes you smile
Summer tastes like strawberries and cream
Summer looks like a bright blue sky with no clouds
Summer is very hot
Summer makes you feel happy.

Jasmine Moss (13)
Churnet View Middle School, Leek

War

War is bad,
War is wrong,
Shooting and stabbing,
Cutting off your tongue.

The Brits Vs the Japs,
We all get slapped,
When the battle is lost
But the war is won.

Fight for your country,
Fight for your land,
If you get bullied, take a stand
Blow off their head with an AK47.

Safety to all,
You can sleep tonight,
No more guns, bombs,
No more midnight fright.

The battle is done
And the war is won.

Matthew Smart (12)
Churnet View Middle School, Leek

Anger

A nger is like lava bubbling inside
N ever going to go until it explodes
G etting as if you will take it out on someone else
E ven if they haven't done anything
R oar! There it goes.
 You'll feel better after.
 Hopefully!

Tracy Drury (13)
Churnet View Middle School, Leek

Wish List

If I had a wish list I would
Climb a mountain high
Fly like a bird in the sky
Have a massive pot of gold
Wish for me and my friends to never grow old
Wish for me and my family to be free
See a monkey in a tree
Wish for my family to be happy
Never have to change a baby's nappy
Shop until I dropped
Wish for my ears to never pop
Send some of my money to Africa
See my family in America
Wish for my wish list to never end . . .

Leanne Sales (13)
Churnet View Middle School, Leek

My Hobby

The bars at the front that help you stay steady,
The tyres on the front
So you can go, ready?
The pedals to help you pick up speed,
The lightweight frame so you can take the lead,
The gears at the rears,
The disc brake on the front,
Jumping a four-foot launch ramp.
Landing with a bump,
Talking to your mates,
About the latest gear.
So if you're into biking
You really have no fear.

Daniel Austin (13)
Churnet View Middle School, Leek

My Cat

My cat's black, ginger and white,
She isn't scary in the night,
She miaows so sweet,
Her fur's all neat
But what's she like underneath?

She's small and cute,
She's lovely and mute,
Her green, bright eyes
Shine like the sun in the sky,
But what's she like underneath?

She's cute when she sleeps,
But she loves to wake for meat,
The smell of food from me and you,
She always wants something new,
But what's she like underneath?

We don't know, we don't really care,
What she likes, she can't share.

Stephanie Robinson (13)
Churnet View Middle School, Leek

The Weather

Rain splashes down in a great big puddle
When all you need is a nice soft cuddle.

The sun comes out to set the scene,
But it reminds me, my sister's still mean.

Snow falls to the ground,
While it doesn't make a sound.

The weather acts like a two-year-old,
Because it won't do as it's told!

Kayleigh Barber (12)
Churnet View Middle School, Leek

Normal Days

Morning's bright, morning's fun,
Time for a juicy hot cross bun.

The sizzling sun and crispy sound,
I decide to watch the 'just passing' band
They play for hours, hours on end,
Until it's time for me to send.

Send myself back inside,
Inside to send my wonders of pride,
I decide to run, run, run, run,
Towards the letter box to fill it with fun.

Until I come back, it will snow, snow again,
And it will wait for me
Until they end the day.

Jamie Duffield (12)
Churnet View Middle School, Leek

Lonely

I am a little fishy, deep in the sea
I've got no friends to come play with me.
I am so lonely and feel so glum.
Why won't anyone come?

I feel like swimming, swimming away,
And hope to find friends who will play.

The sea is glum, glum like me
So the only thing I can do is flee.

Lyndon Birks (13)
Churnet View Middle School, Leek

When I Reach The Golden Age

When I'm old and wrinkly,
And using a wheelchair,
With my big false teeth,
And two chins beneath,
And my curly, permed locks of grey hair,
I'm not gonna show that I'm getting old,
And sit with a grumpy face,
I'm not gonna knit mittens,
And coo over kittens,
Or leave my false teeth 'round the place,
I'm gonna buy a pink motor scooter,
And adopt a fierce bulldog called Butch,
And just for a laugh,
While zooming down the footpath,
Trip people up with my crutch!
I may even try paragliding,
Or surf some unruly waves,
But you never know,
When I pack to go,
Space travel may be the new craze!
When I reach that golden age,
I know it may not be clever,
To hatch such a plot,
But hey, why not?
We're not gonna live forever!

Amy Condrey (13)
Churnet View Middle School, Leek

Fred

There once was a boy called Fred
He looked a bit dead
He ran into town
And got hit by a crown
That fell off the king's head!

Ben Johnson (13)
Churnet View Middle School, Leek

The Dog

He eats your scraps
He jumps all over you
He mucks up your flower bed
He sprays you with water
And slobbers all over you
He gets you up at six
He wees up every post
But most of all
Out of these really,
Really annoying things,
There is one tiny fact
That makes him special and lovable
The way he claws your slippers!

Liam Dukesell (13)
Churnet View Middle School, Leek

Emptiness

My mum left me on the streets to die
Sometimes I wonder and ask myself
Why?
I live in a cardboard box
I can't even afford to buy a pair of
Umbro socks.

I have nobody
Nothing
I'm empty
Empty,
Empty.

Lee Boswell (13)
Churnet View Middle School, Leek

Little Sisters

My little sister is so caring and sweet,
She's a girl who you'd all love to meet,
She's sometimes nice but sometimes mean,
But I am dreading what she'll be like when she is a teen,
When she's moody, she always cries,
She goes to my dad and always lies,
She blames me so I get done,
After we make up and have lots of fun,
But if she wasn't here,
I would cry and drop a tear,
Sisters are lovely,
As long as they don't bug ya.

Amy Corden (13)
Churnet View Middle School, Leek

Life

Life is fresh, life is the smell of summer
Life is easy, as easy as air
Life is precious and cherished by all
Life is the reason why you live
You live to have life
But if life is so amazing, why is it taken away?
Maybe because no one ever actually lives.
Life is fate, life is not real,
If it is, then someone scream!
Life is when you wake up from your dream.

Max Yapp (13)
Churnet View Middle School, Leek

The Shadow People

They lurk!
They lurk in the shadows.

They hide!
They bide their time watching you.

Are they people of the past?
Or spirits harassed?

They see!
They see you now!

So be careful of what you do
The shadow people are watching you.

Elliott Goldstraw (13)
Churnet View Middle School, Leek

My Pets

My dog Archie, he is really cute
Then there's my cat Tiggy, really quiet and mute
They're like brothers, cool in their fur
The dog is scruffy and the cat just purrs.
Eating dry dog food and all the tuna
The more you give them, the fatter they get.
Archie is my puppy, Tiggy is my cat
There's one thing that's true, you cannot change that.

Ryan Burkitt (13)
Churnet View Middle School, Leek

An Otter's Day

Across the louring, dismal water,
Awakening none, for none do stir,
Over the pebble bed,
Like a velvet shadow phantom,
Sneaking through the shadows,
Fast and light, he glides below,
Swiftly he then dives down deep,
Brushing his fur across the scratching claws of pebbles.
He sneaks upon his prey,
Invisible to all who do not see,
Here and there it moves once over,
A slashing move! His meal is done.
As he rises to the silk surface,
He moves gently over the top,
Separating the lilies from the lilies,
A wandering stranger over the surface,
Defining his way in a selective path,
Rolling ripples over and over,
Gliding around like a gentle swan,
Swimming forward on his front,
Moving to a piece of music,
Full of grace and elegance,
With every movement of his tail,
Smoothly he slips and skims,
Till he moves on back to be swallowed,
Gulped up by the flowing hair of weed,
To lie like a shadow of non-existence.

Rebecca Thomas (14)
Derby High School, Littleover

The Listeners (From Their Perspective)

(Inspired by 'The Listeners' by Walter de la Mare)

'Listen to him calling,' said the listeners,
Looking through the dark windowpane,
'He disturbs us with his knocking,
We wish he would refrain.
He comes upon this moonlit hour,
When EastEnders has just begun,
Doesn't he know Dot Cotton's
Been reunited with her son?
We listen to him calling,
And silently we stay,
The telly's turned to mute,
We wish he'd go away!
A hundred years spent listening,
Within these silent walls,
It's enough to drive you crazy,
No wonder we watch Thunder Balls,
And now he's here *bashing,*
Filling up all the air,
With his promises and mutterings,
Which echo up our stairs,
Finally he stops a-knocking,
And revs his horse to go,
Thank goodness he's given up the ghost,
Now we can listen to our show!'

Leah Beardmore (14)
Derby High School, Littleover

Butterfly

At first, I didn't know what it was
Sitting on the windshield of the still-hot car
It spread its wings out, and then I saw
Scarlet-red, tipped with black
And the opposite on the lower wings
This ying-yang creature, beautiful in every respect
From its graceful ballerina legs
To its wings, like the smallest, smoothest, glossiest of feathers
And its body, like the tiniest of black painted twigs.

It could have been no more than an inch wide
And one long, and it had danced in the air
Like a coloured rendition of Swan Lake
And it came to rest, probably as tired as I
Marvelling at the sheer baking heat of this mid-June evening
And the brightness the sun cast upon the dull colour of England.

It lay, resting in the heat
Sun worshipping like any beauty queen
Those amazing wings, those feats of nature
Gently moving up and down, as though fanning
It was too hot to move fast
Then, once more, its flight was flattened against the glass
And the butterfly sprang
Into the air
And out of my reach . . .

Lauren Bond (14)
Derby High School, Littleover

No Letting Go

Why am I so scared?
Why am I full of fear?
All I can think is the worst
Right now, right here.
The wind is blowing
Blowing in my face
The only thing I know
Is that he has gone to a better place.
I loved him
I loved him so, so much
His lovely kind words
His soft gentle touch
I miss him so, badly
Especially when I come home
There is nobody waiting for me
I am all alone.
Sometimes I wonder
Why God has taken him from me
I really want him to be here
I wish everyone could see.
I wish for a miracle
Or one simple wish
So I could bring him back to me
Just for one last kiss.
The only problem is
This could not come true
So I have to move on
Even though I will remember you!

Daisy Williams (14)
Derby High School, Littleover

Tiger

Veins of black streaking across orange velvet,
A roar that could shred bone, cuts through the silence
Of the moonlit night.
The hunter gasps as the growl grapples and grips at his throat,
His breath is lost in the blackness of the night.
The hunter is the hunted.

Except the tables can turn,
A bullet pierces the calm,
The tiger tightens, tenses, holds,
Then all that can be seen is a shadow flitting and weaving
Through the trees,
Sewing fear into the fabric of life.

Appliquéd onto the cloak of dead night, two lights ignite.
Amber to the eye,
But black to the soul.
Followed by a mass of rippling muscle,
A lean killing machine that captures the heart of all,
Wears boxing gloves equipped with claws.
Then, it's over . . .

Pearl razor teeth,
Tainted with prey's red essence.
Corpse eyes burn as it stares up at the
wondrous beast.
The antenna-like ears swivel, picking up a
signal.
Deep in the foliage.
A writhing, slicing, slithering snake whips
through the air,
As the tiger exits, becoming a whisper on
the winds.

A lord
Beautiful to the eye,
But dangerous to the heart.

Rebecca Bussey (14)
Derby High School, Littleover

The Crow

As black as night, the crow patrols his territory,
Jabbing his talons into the defenceless earth,
Shrieking to make himself heard,
Yet left all alone to wander.

Rotates his head around his body,
Lifts his small wings and floats gracefully into the motionless air.
He gently flaps his wings as he examines the ground beneath him
Suddenly he swoops downwards.

He sees the fear in his prey's eyes,
As he plunges to the ground,
The feeble worm is gripped securely into the crow's claws,
Terrorised and unaware of its fate.

The crow loosens his grip as he reaches the ground
And attacks the unconscious worm with his razor-sharp beak.
The dastardly deed is done,
And once again, he guards his ground awaiting his next strike.

Lizzie Saunders (14)
Derby High School, Littleover

Just Imagine!

Imagine being a drama teacher
It would be better than being a preacher
Dressing like Depp acting like Bloom
Singing like Mariah Carey in an ancient tomb.
Singing along, the beat goes ding dong,
Oh how I can't wait
God thank you for making life
Oh so great!

Niki Thomas (12)
Four Dwellings High School, Quinton

Best Days Of Our Life

They are the best days of our life
It's what people say
Do your very best
And try your hardest every day.

Teachers are strict, teachers are kind,
Teachers are helpful all of the time.

Classrooms are big, classrooms are small
Classrooms, small and some are swell.

Teachers are strict, teachers are kind,
Teachers are helpful all of the time.

Thursdays are art, English, maths, PE and science,
A busy day from Four Dwellings High School.

Teachers are strict, teachers are kind,
Teachers are helpful all of the time.

In times of trouble, in times of need,
You can count on the teachers to always lead
A showing hand, a caring thought,
A kind gesture of their support.

Teachers are strict, teachers are kind,
Teachers are helpful all of the time.

Alisha Myatt (13)
Four Dwellings High School, Quinton

A Spell To Be A Successful Football Player

To be a successful football player act in the right way,
Try your hardest every day.
You need to be able to strike the ball
Don't be afraid, just stand up tall.
To always be the one scoring goals
Just hit the ball in-between the poles.
So you don't get injured in every way
Do your exercises every day.
To be a good footballer you will need lots of skills
So you earn lots of money to pay the bills.
To win every single game
Work together and put the other team to shame.
All you will have to do is work hard with the team,
So that you can live your dream.

Paul Cashmore (12)
Four Dwellings High School, Quinton

The War Poem

I am sitting in this horrible, cold trench
I feel really hungry and sad
At the moment I feel like I am going to wrench
This whole situation is getting really mad
Two days ago I went over the top
I was really glad that I survived
But I was also sad because my friend got shot.

My friend was a wonderful man
He fought for our country well
When the Germans shot him, all we heard was *boom!*
Even though my friend is dead in my head
He will always be my best pal.

So this is all about me and the war
Forever in our thoughts for evermore . . .

Michelle Pike (13)
Four Dwellings High School, Quinton

Angel Poem

Golden curls and ocean-blue eyes,
A smell as sweet as honey,
Her voice as soft as the whisper of the breeze,
Her wings are as soft as a baby's skin.

A beautiful light is all around her,
She holds out her delicate hand to me,
'Do not worry,' she says to me,
'You'll be safe with us.'

She laughs like she's singing,
I can hear my heart hammering in my chest,
Like a horse's hooves when he's running on the grass,
I took her hand and we slowly floated from the ground.

I took her other hand and she smiled at me gently,
We went in slow circles in mid-air,
Other angels appeared too,
Slowly we drifted away into the unknown,
Soon out of sight, never to be seen again . . .

Maisy Moran (12)
Four Dwellings High School, Quinton

My Dragon

My pet dragon is big and red,
Although I must say he is a pain in the head.
He's always flying around,
He's never on the ground.
I always look after my dragon,
But he thinks it's a con.
The one thing he's scared of is a mouse,
So he comes to me and hides in the house.
I really love my dragon.

My dragon has a lot of scales,
He never ever tells tales.
My dragon's stomach is so big,
I think he must have eaten a pig.
My dragon is so strong,
And so is his great big pong.
My dragon has big sharp claws,
I bet they're even bigger than yours.
My dragon is as big as a school,
Doesn't my dragon rule?

Tristan Dyas (13)
Four Dwellings High School, Quinton

A Spell To Be A Successful Archaeologist

If you wanna be successful in archaeology,
Read this poem and you will begin to see,
That archaeology is incredibly easy!
So cast the spell now and be home for tea.

You need to add a huge spade,
To find out where the bodies are laid,
Discovering new places to play hide-and-seek,
Inside the burial, it's cold and bleak.

I look inside, there are only pots and plates,
A few fruit bowls filled with mouldy dates,
I look around, I am very disappointed,
Then I spot the remains of a mummified kid.

Now place all this within the pot,
All the information, which seems to be a lot,
Then mix in a handful of sand,
And now you are the best archaeologist of the land!

Rosie Dawes (12)
Four Dwellings High School, Quinton

To Be A Successful Student

Concentrate on your work in class,
In your test make sure you pass.
Always listen to the teacher,
A better brain will always hit ya.
Never lose on the sports day,
Don't skive off with a holiday!

Always be proud of what you've got,
Do lots of sums to solve the plot.
Get your spelling always right,
Never do the work in the night.
In DT you have to cook,
In English you have to read a book.

About your work, never say no,
Always be cool and your mind will grow.

Jake Moroney (12)
Four Dwellings High School, Quinton

The Sun

The sun is like a big tangerine
It's as hot as the Sahara Desert
It revolves like a disco ball
It is as exciting as a theme park
It burns me to the bone like molten magma
It is an orange Red Leicester
It smells like a bonfire.

It is as interesting as camping out
It crackles like Rice Krispies.

Matthew Jackson (12)
Hagley Park Sports College, Rugeley

In Response To Sylvia Plath's 'Mirror'

(Inspired by 'Mirror' by Sylvia Plath)

I am clear and free. I have no owner.
Wherever I go it's never the same.
I can mould myself around the simplest of forms
And swallow them immediately
Just as it is unmissed by love or dislike.
Most of the time I travel round twisted banks;
They are brown and muddy.
I have been with them so long
I think that they are part heart.
But it flickers; shadows and reflections hover over me.

Now I am a mirror. A woman bends over me
Searching the deepest, darkest depths of me
Looking for the real her, sending ripples all over me.
She rewards me with tears and agitation of hand.
I am important to her. She comes and goes.
In me she has drowned a young girl,
And in me an old woman rises towards her
Day after day like a terrible plague.

Lorna Chilton (15)
Hagley Park Sports College, Rugeley

Heart's Discontent

The splendour of life holds me no more,
There's a feeling inside me I've not felt before.
I've given up, I can't go on,
The days are boring, the nights are long.
I have no want, I feel no need,
This heart of mine - it starts to bleed.
A crimson river of regret
Sadly won't let me forget,
The things I feel, the things I've seen
Reflect on me by what I've been.
People don't notice, they never see,
The pain and hatred flowing through me.

Rob Earle (15)
Hagley Park Sports College, Rugeley

Too Many Women!

There are too many women!
Women spread gossip
Women pollute the air
Women consume five times their own body weight
In perfume a week.
Women were worshipped in decadent societies
(London and New York town).
The Greeks had more use of women.
Women sit down to pee (too lazy to stand up)
Perhaps they are alright in their own world,
But their traditions are alien to ours.
In this world the superior race should be male,
Women in another world if they want!

Kevin Guy (15)
Hagley Park Sports College, Rugeley

Silence

Everything is quiet,
Everything is still,
Nothing moving,
Nothing speaking,
Everything is peaceful,
You can even hear,
A pin drop on the floor,
Or a tiny mouse squeak,
As it comes through the door,
You can hear the blackbird sing,
His beautiful song in the distance,
It is all so quiet
All so silent.

Sam Gunby (15)
Hagley Park Sports College, Rugeley

Consumers' Report

I saw it in the market
It felt great to start with,
But after a while the feeling went
In fact it was a real anticlimax
It's called love.
In my view it's overpriced
But we all have different opinions
I rolled the bottle between my hands
And felt the contents move
It was thick and deep.
It doesn't have a sell-by date
But for some it only works for a few days.
It's a very deceptive thing.
People think it will be a great feeling
But then they use it too much
And end up in a mess.
I'm glad to report it had a warning on -
Can cause loss of life.
It was printed in black and yellow capitals
I saw that this wasn't the first version
Humanity's had millions of years to get it right
Well I'd buy it
But give it a few goes first.
You're bound to get it right sometime
But the question of 'best buy'
I'd like to leave until I get
The competitive product you said you'd send.

Alan Malpass (15)
Hagley Park Sports College, Rugeley

For A Moment

I saw for just a moment,
Your little arms and legs,
The little blur they said was you,
But now you've gone away.
I heard for just a moment,
The beating of your heart,
The sound that held such promise,
But soon it would depart.
I dreamt for just a moment,
Of the day I'd hold you tight,
I'd listen for your little breath,
And rock you through the night.
I cried for just a moment,
When they said that you had gone.
I laid alone in silence,
Which seemed so very long
I prayed for just a moment,
That you would be reborn,
Into my arms you would come and forever would be warm.
I was for just a moment,
The mother of a child,
Who laughed and cried and meant so much,
If only for a while.
In that single moment,
When I finally said farewell,
I knew that we would meet again, little baby,
For time will only tell.

Michelle Whitty (15)
Hagley Park Sports College, Rugeley

Boys

There will be no more boys
Boys spread infection
Boys pollute the air,
Boys consume seven times
Their own weight in food a week.
Well that's a bit exaggerated but it's something like that.
Boys stand up to pee,
Perhaps they are alright in their own country
But they are like aliens to me.
Boys smell, especially after sport,
Boys watch too much television.
They can sleep through anything,
And they always stab me in the back.
'It's not you, it's me,'
'I think I just like you as a friend,'
Two of their favourite sayings.
The problem is I still like him, I still want him
I still need him
He's got my love
He has got my heart
My babe, my sweetie, my love,
My Mr Right!

Yasmin Follows (14)
Hagley Park Sports College, Rugeley

Grandpa

You were my special grandpa
You were always there for me.
Reading me a story,
And sitting on your knee.

Then at the age of nine,
It suddenly came to me
You weren't going to read me a story
Sitting on your knee.

Cancer hit your body
Cancer hit me too
I didn't really know
I didn't have a clue.

It was time for you to go,
Time to say goodbye,
'Please don't leave us Grandpa,
We know we're going to cry!'

We love you dearly Tom,
Don't leave us, this is torture,
But here's a loving message,
From your darling, your granddaughter.

Charlotte Blackford (14)
Hagley Park Sports College, Rugeley

True Insanity

Donne, is the idea of halting the sun
To stop time to be poetic
Marvell, to the idea of talking for an age
About a Lady's arm in lam's.
Larkin, is a man who on his wedding night
Declares his persona a woman
Declaring to the world you feel guilty about
Life in a mixture of things.

These geniuses with their own corner!
Who would ever see a chance to ridicule
Oh grateful colours, bright looks;
Oh grateful fire, bright burns
If only the Laurette had a mirror.
Which had more to behold than the wall opposite!
Only this breed of insanity would
Spend hours writing eight lines, no one else
Understands!

Put them in a forest - you'll have the
Beauty of nature and the chill of the night.
Put them in a desert you'll have
Metaphors of empty lives and vast eternity.
Only a delinquent mind would see an
Ocean of ice as a field of fire.
How would anyone ever
Aim, desire, strive to be a poet?

Daniel Pyatt (15)
Hagley Park Sports College, Rugeley

Unknown, Untouched, Unseen

Your sparkling blue eyes, almost like the sky above,
The sky lacking the affection
Shown by these amazing features.
Your voice is sensational, ringing constantly in my ears,
Lingering only to remind me of your kind and gentle ways.
Your smile is warm, showing love to all things seen.
Your presence is what I long for every minute of the day.
But to my disappointment,
I can only dream of the time that we could be together.
I'd love to run my fingers through your silky blonde hair
That flows ever so gently free,
Delicately framing your fragile face that beams with joy.

Your humour delights me, it will obtain my attention always,
You act with concern for all creatures
And long to portray a positive message to all people.
I see your face only in school,
But long to reach out and touch your tender heart.
My mind secures a picture of you so that we will never be apart.

Ryan Hicks (14)
Hagley Park Sports College, Rugeley

The Battlefields

Bloodstained and hurting, death is all around,
Twisted and mangled corpses lie upon my ground,
My flowers are dead, trampled and distraught,
Man was so peaceful, or at least so I thought
Once upon a time I flourished with life.
Now covered in chaos, guns, sword and knife.
I would give anything just to hear the birds sing
To watch them fly, soar and take wing,
I'm nothing, I'm worthless, all I am is a field,
But forever I shall stand, an everlasting shield.

Ayla Smythe (14)
Haywood School, Sherwood

The Battlefield

My field used to be green grass with the sun shining over.
That's all gone now, nothing but dirt and remains of the
innocent victims.

The pictures I have seen are very disturbing,
Men that have a mother and father just killed for nothing.
Maybe they have sweethearts,
The soldiers have no defence, just basic clothing.

The field never seems to be quiet anymore
Even at night it's just the dreadful noises, *bang, bang!*
Oh no!
Another innocent victim has been killed.

There was one man, I remember so very well.
Such a young boy, not old enough to vote, but old enough to fight
in the war!
He gave one last despairing look then shot at the enemy.
Bang, bang!
The young, innocent boy was gone.

Elisha Edwards (14)
Haywood School, Sherwood

Battlefield . . .

Once a green body
So full of brightness
Now covered in dead and mud.
Noises stop
Last man tumbles,
Now he's gone for good.

The soundless atmosphere
Takes me back
Before this war began
I'm green
I'm colourful
I'm where the children ran.

Bang, bang, bang,
It brings me back
To this unforgiving earth
Thud, thud, thud,
It's on again
I'm a battlefield, for all it's worth.

Claire Johnson (13)
Haywood School, Sherwood

The Battlefield!

I sit here alone
All by myself
Lonely, as usual
As I sit beyond the weary blue sky
Fresh green grass groans on top of me
That felt perfect until that one day . . .

Footsteps trampled on me
As blood penetrated through me
English killing Germans
All happened on top of me
Shrapnel dissipates all around the cold, hateful, autumn air.
Hitting the floor in a vogue
Bodies plummet in groups of 2, 3, 4, never to end.

The war air is fading now
War is nearly over
November the 11th is the day war is predicted over
At last!

Poppies now that grow
Are the remembrance of all the soldiers that died in the war.

Jade Hoppis (14)
Haywood School, Sherwood

Life After Death

The war is over,
So is my life.
My son and husband are dead,
Now I'm a widow.
My daughter is always filled with tears
An endless waterfall full of emotions.
When the night draws near I dread the thought
Of those feelings I feel and having to sleep on my own,
All I can hear are the screams and cries of the raging winds.
Then suddenly that soul-twisting day comes,
When I have to lay to rest the two most important men
In my life
And I feel weakened, sickened to my stomach.
But how I would love to see how our leaders feel now,
Now they have won the war,
Feeling proud to be English.
I am ashamed to even admit my nationality.
To think only if they could just keep out,
That my son and husband would be here,
Happy at home with us.
Then yes, we would all love to say we're English
So you tell me,
Are *you* proud to be English?

Sharna Reedman (14)
Haywood School, Sherwood

The Battlefield

I was green, I was brown until I felt a soldier's boot
Touch my ground.

I was healthy, I was clean until I heard the voice of
The first man scream.

I was happy, never glum until I felt a hot hell
From a soldier's gun.

I used to have roses growing on me,
Now blood is the only thing red I can see.

I used to be surrounded by children playing,
Now all I can feel is pain.

Then one day it stopped, it finished,
And my roots slowly started to replenish.

Kennedy Williams (14)
Haywood School, Sherwood

A Cat Trapped In A Shed

Searching through the grotty window
Looking to and fro,
For anyone who is kind enough
To come and let me go.

Jumping off the windowpane,
Staring at the floor,
Why doesn't someone come up
To the shed and open up the door?

I hear footsteps all the time,
Why can't they see?
I am here all alone,
Why can't they set me free?

Priya Minhas (12)
Hodge Hill Girls' School, Birmingham

Help Me, I'm Being Bullied!

Sitting down all alone,
Wondering if they'll come to my home,
I think they'll get me when I'm at school,
The bullies are the ones that always look cool,
I reckon they probably got bullied themselves,
That is why they bully me myself,
I should really tell someone.
An adult, teacher, Dad or Mum,
I shouldn't run away from this,
If I get help I can beat it,
I should be able to walk tall,
But people bully me because I am small.
It's like a deep, dark tunnel and I can't find the way,
I thought hard and long,
I know what I've got to say,
Can you stop them bullying me
So I can become free?

Louise Heath (13)
Hodge Hill Girls' School, Birmingham

Deepest Shadows

Nowhere to run
Nowhere to hide
No way to cover my battered pride
As deep as the night
As calm as the sea
Running around trying to capture me
The closer it gets, the harder to see
This horrid thing that is after me
Full of fear, my heart it bleeds
Shall I run or shall I cry?
No matter which one
I'm still going to die.

Natalie Green (13)
Hodge Hill Girls' School, Birmingham

The Scream Under My Bed

At bedtime, I went upstairs,
On the pillow, I lay my head.
Then the voice came back to me.
The scream under my bed.

I lay wide awake, waiting,
To hear the voice again,
But I took a sigh of relief
As in came my brother, Ben.

He sat on my bed and
Asked me if everything was alright.
I nodded my head instead of saying yes,
Because my throat felt very tight.

He got up from my bed
And walked towards the door
Before I knew what I was doing,
I jumped onto the floor.

I knew what I should do
I knew what was right
So I bent down my head
And looked at the feared sight.

My heart filled with happiness
As I saw who was touching my head.
It had whiskers and went *miaow!*
This was the scream under my bed.

Aisha Ghafoor (12)
Hodge Hill Girls' School, Birmingham

The Ghost

There was a ghost
So white and large
I wouldn't touch him
Wearing camouflage.

He haunts the hall
All through the night
He wakes us up
And gives us a fright.

He killed the dog
He killed the cat
I saw him move
Oh, it's just a rat.

He closed the curtains
He moved the bed,
The walls were white,
Now they're red.

He turned off the TV
He switched it back on
He scared the neighbours
Now they're gone.

He still haunts the hall
He killed my cat
He's scaring me now
Let's move to a flat.

Christine Rice (12)
Hodge Hill Girls' School, Birmingham

Our Deadly Relationship

Not once did I try to break away
I was needy and she promised me
She wouldn't bully me about my weight
So I stayed, eventually
She kept piercing me every day
She didn't care that I would bleed
Torturing me until I would say
Bulimia, I don't want my feed.

The only thing I knew, I thought
Was bulimia was who I was
· I loved her, I never fought
She hated me, and would haunt
Me every day, in my sleep
I would wake shivering
Cold,
She used to keep me
Locked away, dying.

Anam Khan (14)
Hodge Hill Girls' School, Birmingham

Flower Flower

Flower, flower grow for me
Become a flower from a seed,
Grow your roots and a stem,
Let the water come right in.

Flower, flower you are true,
You make me happy when I am blue,
You became a flower from a seed,
You did all that just for me.

Maariyah Khan (12)
Hodge Hill Girls' School, Birmingham

I'm Not Lying

I saw a giant in my back garden
It was flying,
I'm not lying.

I saw Superman in my back garden,
He was crying
I'm not lying.

I saw Mariah Carey in my back garden,
She was sighing,
I'm not lying.

I saw McFly in my back garden,
They were whining,
I'm not lying.

I saw my dad in my back garden,
He was ironing,
I'm not lying.

Zakia Sultana (12)
Hodge Hill Girls' School, Birmingham

The Flower!

They can be artificial or real,
They are soft and smooth when you feel 'em
Different shades and sizes they come in,
Different seeds and soils they grow in
Roses and daffodils are one of 'em
But roses are the most popular one of all of 'em
They can be small to hide behind a tower,
Guess what it is? Yes, it's a flower!

Nazmeen Akhtar (12)
Hodge Hill Girls' School, Birmingham

The Path To Love

(This poem is for all the people who I loved that have died)

My love for you was in the air, it was everywhere.
My love for you was like a rose blossoming in the midsummer night.
Your love for me touched my heart and never let us be apart.
Love was ours and always will be.
We used to fly like birds, hand in hand, heart in heart.
Every night in my dreams I feel you, I see you.
Every second, every minute, every hour, every day, every night
I knew you would have been there for me.
You showed me the path of love.
You showed me the beauty that I possessed inside of me.
You were the only one to fulfil my needs.
The day you died, my heart sank.
My love for you had drowned in my blood.
People wanted to see you for the last time when you were
                                                            in the coffin.
They were pushing and shoving, I couldn't take any of it.
I knew if I wanted to meet you, I'd find our secret place in my heart.
Who's gonna love me when I get up?
I know you will wherever you are.
I know our love will live forever.
I know our souls will be together.
For every flower that opens, for every birds that sings,
For every deed of kindness, for every little word of love . . .
I had a few I would have said before you died.

I love you!

Halima Hafeez (13)
Hodge Hill Girls' School, Birmingham

Friends In Need

Friends in need are friends indeed
Friends share, friends care
Friends advise, never tell lies.
Friends are who you trust,
Friends will never follow their passions and lusts.

Friends will always tell you to do good,
As their hearts tell you to do as you should.
Friends are there when you are happy or sad,
Friends are happy to share your happiness or joy.
Your hearts are attached as one, as gold, as they always had.
My friend and I were best friends when I was a little girl.
Now we are old, shoulder to shoulder, hand clasped in hand.

Friends are daffodils in spring.
Like a diamond encrusted in a silver ring.

Friends travel with you in your journey of life
Friends stroll side by side
Friends are those who help you on the path to paradise,
Yes, true friendship is all this, which will never go to sighs.

Saima Jokhia (13)
Hodge Hill Girls' School, Birmingham

Waiting

Waiting, waiting, always waiting
Waiting for my mum
Waiting on the doorstep, heated by the sun.
Waiting for your smile, waiting for your hugs,
I've been waiting for a long time
Since you've been gone.

Bethany Shannahan (11)
Hodge Hill Girls' School, Birmingham

Fading Friend

I once had a friend
Who said our friendship would never end.
She is now far away doing things a different way
I don't know why she had to go
And leave me all alone
In a faraway, distant home.
I guess she was fading away
In another world where she has to stay
She never even said goodbye
She has flown away like a kite
I guess she was put to test
And is now laying down to rest
I now know she is fading away
Why did our friendship break
When it took a long time to make?
We have to stay strong but I wonder
Why we were wrong
I will always remember.

Azadi Mir (12)
Hodge Hill Girls' School, Birmingham

Poem

A river of laughter is full of joy,
Laughter of love, friendship and life.
When the river doesn't flow,
Your life goes slow.
The reason of this river is your love for your family.
Without a family your life is dark and dull,
Never live life alone,
Family are with you in your journey of life,
Never leave them.

Samaira Begum (12)
Hodge Hill Girls' School, Birmingham

Someone Special

Down to Earth, you have come,
To feed us, to kiss us, to slap our bum!
You took care of us when we were small,
You made sure that we would never fall.
You cured all of our dreadful diseases,
Slimy snots, sore throats, colds and sneezes!
What would we do without you?
You taught us how to use the loo!
Although you can be annoying some of the time,
But to leave you would be the biggest crime.
It would be sad if you weren't here,
It would be our biggest fear!

Down to Earth, you have come,
We always knew you were number one!

My mum!

Imtisal Ul-Haq (12)
Hodge Hill Girls' School, Birmingham

A Poem For You

You are the sight of a stem growing,
Slowly, day by day,
Rising from the ground,
Into a beautiful flower,
You are the smell of freshness,
Of a lovely spring day.
You are the taste,
Of a red, juicy strawberry.
You are the touch of a rabbit's fur
For you I should like to take,
That star that lies,
Between the sky,
And the magic of the moon.

Farhat Naeem (12)
Hodge Hill Girls' School, Birmingham

Africa

A beautiful place
A wonderful nation
The only disgrace
Is that they pay for education.
Poor children who can't
Afford to go to school
Sit at the gates
And plead for a change in the rules.
Teachers refuse
They say they need to pay staff
It's their only excuse.
Children break-in
Teachers find out
Give them a slap
A lecture and a shout.
Children with no homes
Sit on the street
With rags for clothes
And injured, bare feet.
They have to pay up
But they cannot afford
So they sit on the street
And pray to their Lord.

Faiza Qasim (12)
Hodge Hill Girls' School, Birmingham

My Sister

I can be a pain,
But my older sister won't let it rain.
I have to confess,
That she is the best.
She is like my friend
This sister-sister friendship will never end.

When I'm in trouble,
We become double.
She has the key to success,
Our love between us will never be less.
When I'm down,
She'll come down as a clown.

She's the best,
This is no test.
She's just great,
She's my best mate.

I have learnt a lot with her,
Skin soft as fur.
She's everything to me,
You just have to see.

Henna Hussain (12)
Hodge Hill Girls' School, Birmingham

Untitled

You're all the world to me you know,
And when you go away,
The sun goes out, the clouds come down,
And all the world is grey.

You're every single thing to me,
Your voice, your look, your touch,
When you are cross with me it hurts,
I can't explain how much.

So even when you let me down,
I know you really won't,
I'll still put all my trust in you

And show you that I care.

Faybian Taylor (12)
Hodge Hill Girls' School, Birmingham

The Mosque!

As I come in,
I hear this sound!
People are here
So I look around.

People are bowing,
I see their faces,
There are so many of them,
Praying for mercy and grace.

Scented sticks,
Smell so fair
Spreading their scent,
Across the air.

Now I'm leaving,
Very slow,
With all the memories,
Which will never go!

Siara Nawaz (12)
Hodge Hill Girls' School, Birmingham

Friendship

Friendship is a bond between strangers that met
Not knowing they would end up together
Not knowing they would be the ones who'd go through
The good, the bad and the tough.
That they were the ones who'd share happiness and love.

Friendship is a bond that is different to lovers and enemies.
Lovers' love, they don't give up for their partners,
But friends do
That's what different friendship is about.
When you know you are lifelong friends
You can forgive no matter how big their mistake is.
You can sacrifice and give a shoulder for them to cry on
They laugh, they cry, they always remain . . .
Together.

Mewish Hussain (12)
Hodge Hill Girls' School, Birmingham

My End Of Term Poem

Hurrah! Wicked!
School is out,
Time to play and mess about.
When it's over, give us a shout,
See ya in six weeks – chill-out!

Play out with my mates, climb up trees
Have loads of ice cream *argh! Brainfreeze,*
Piping hot, gonna get a tan,
Have fun the best way I can.

Clothes shopping, buying shoes,
I don't know which ones to choose.
Summer holidays are great, it's true,
I've spent half talking to you!

Courtnii Welch (12)
Hodge Hill Girls' School, Birmingham

Hallowe'en Night!

Everyone's excited,
Wearing spooky costumes,
Running around, hyper,
Collecting candy sweets.

Dressed as witches,
Spiders, bats and mummies,
Knocking on doors,
For more candy sweets.

Stuffing candy in their mouths,
And asking for more.
Sharing all the candy sweets,
For one and more.

The night has nearly ended,
Children are getting tired,
Parents shouting, 'Bedtime!'
And off they go to sleep.

Amreen Ali (12)
Hodge Hill Girls' School, Birmingham

My Special Ring

I have a special ring
It shines; *bling-bling!*
It glistens in the light
And it shines very bright.

My mum gave it to me
It's so special, can't you see?
It shows all the love she has given
And all the love she has forbidden.
All the things I've done wrong
I hope I'm forgiven.
Only I can see the magic within
I'll never throw it in the bin.

My special ring.

Atiyah Ghulam (12)
Hodge Hill Girls' School, Birmingham

Cat Near Heaven

A cat's small world is full of dreams,
Of full food balls and scents unseen,
Of open fields and a cosy chair,
And most of all of you standing there.

And when the end is drawing near,
And you are trying to stop your tears,
She licks your hand with a happy sigh,
Happy that you are standing by.

When she reaches Heaven's gate,
The Lord says, 'Come,' but she says, 'Wait,
I have a friend I love so dear
And I can feel her footsteps near.'

Your lifetime's passed, you're near God's throne.
One happy glance, you're not alone,
Your loving pet, so patient waits,
To pass with you through Heaven's gates.

Maryam Aziz (12)
Hodge Hill Girls' School, Birmingham

The Tsunami

The sea is a peaceful and dreamy sight
A delicate breeze blows against you gently
When you dip your hand into it
It becomes drops of pure diamonds
Then all of a sudden, in the twinkle of an eye
Come waves that can reach the sky
Thrashing, churning, coiling madly
The sea raises as high as the clouds
Turning the fluffy white into mad darkness
As it rushes forth
It terrorizes whatever it swallows
Once it reaches the land
It will not leave a trace of mercy behind.

Nadia Ali (13)
Hodge Hill Girls' School, Birmingham

Kids

'Sit up straight,'
Said Mum to Mabel
'Keep your elbows
Off the table.
Do not eat peas
Off a fork.
Your mouth is full,
Don't try and talk.
Keep your mouth shut
When you eat.
Keep still or you'll
Fall off your seat.
If you want more,
You will say 'Please'.
Don't fiddle with
That piece of cheese!'
If, then, we kids,
Cause such a fuss,
Why do you go on
Knowing us?

Uzma Hussain (12)
Hodge Hill Girls' School, Birmingham

A Piece Of History

An elderly piece of earth,
That will never be deceased
As strong as an ox,
It will never break in two.
Sat in soil for most of its days.
Separated now to sleep in peace.
Rough as sandpaper,
Smoothness it lacks,
But it survives without it,
For it's a piece of *history*.

Daniel Wright (13)
Kimberley School, Kimberley

Gone

As young as the morning sun
Born just months ago
Eyes as big as a full moon
Wishing she didn't have to go so soon
Mountain-top ears
As pointy as the stars
Her smell so strong
Like roses on a summer's day
A long tail the length of a jungle vine
Fur as smooth as water, and as black as the night's sky,
Yet as white as a snowflake.
Whiskers long and thin to guide her up to Heaven's cloud
And now she sleeps with the stars
She's gone, no way we can bring her back.

Lucy Atkinson (13)
Kimberley School, Kimberley

My Teacher Doesn't Like Me

My teacher does not like me,
He beats me out of glee.
Poked me with my pencil,
And stole my favourite stencil.

My teacher does not like me
He always gives me a 'D'
I never need to stop and say,
Do I have detention today?

My teacher does not like me,
I'm never home for tea,
If my poems do not rhyme,
I'm kept in all lunchtime.

James Smith (14)
Kimberley School, Kimberley

Old Creature Of The Seabed

The grey clay has seen many things
Scraping, scratching, smoothing on the sea floor
When you look at it, your mind spins around
Around, around, around like a merry-go-round
Pick it up, it's heavy and smooth
Ridged and weathered like an old sea boat
What used to be a creature is now just a piece of rock
Mounted on a yellow wood base
It has taken two million years for this masterpiece to form
You could sit and watch it for all your life
And it would not change.
Lonely on its own, no friends
Every so often someone may take a look at it
But no one will know just what this fossil has seen.

James Salinger (13)
Kimberley School, Kimberley

Old Rock

Grey as a rainy day,
Weathered old fishing boat,
As knobbly as a golf ball,
A sticky roll of sellotape,
Flush as a piece of silk,
Layered piece of slate,
A swirly helter-skelter,
Smells of varnish,
On wood it sits in blissful nothingness,
In ruin, it remains, disregarded by previous proprietors,
Full of memories from long, long ago.

Peter Mossendew (13)
Kimberley School, Kimberley

Brass Angel

Engravings rough yet in the same way, smooth,
Mountain ridges and exquisite grooves.
Royal crest, a symbol old,
Labradors and cornfields drenched in gold.
Decus et Tutamen, inscription ancient.
The Queen's head lies there, solemn and patient.
As opaque as a planet standing still
Lonely and cold enough to chill.
Shiny like the sun on water with the light of the moon,
Round like a chicken's egg born too soon.
Pocket to pocket, passed in through generations,
Standing proud, the currency of our nation.

William Weightman (13)
Kimberley School, Kimberley

Untitled

Lifeless and light,
Backbone crippled,
Its veins like dead riverbeds,
Its skin nets the light
Delicate and fragile,
Little, golden-brown cover.
Half curved edge like a humpback bridge,
Some ladybird spots,
Jagged edge to protect itself from predators.
The spider sees the blue sky from under it
Until it is blown away,
Lands on a beach,
Camouflaged by the sand,
The dead holly leaf lies down.

Megan Ocheduszko (13)
Kimberley School, Kimberley

The Pink Cravat!

Baby-pink petals
Like a newborn piglet,
What a perfect cravat,
This rose would make,
A strong stalk,
The backbone of the flower,
Lea ding up to the star-shaped cradle,
Holding up the face of this perfect plant,
The veiny leaves
An old man's arm,
Hold up the droplets of rain on a stormy day,
The jagged edges of the pure green leaves,
The tip of a fence in a backyard,
Pure green lime fruits
Ripe and sweet,
Stands out from the rest,
Four small buds,
Peeking out of their shells,
Like a baby in a blanket,
The smell is pure,
Fresh and sweet,
The scent of the petals
Strong like love,
The petals,
Silky and smooth
Like the wings of an angel
Sent down from above.

Tia Denby (13)
Kimberley School, Kimberley

Fred

In a field, munching grass,
Watching all the birds pass;
With eyes that sadden every heart;
Another 'lawnmower' doing his part.
Just standing where no man goes,
His tragic tales that no one knows.
To one patch of grass and then the next;
Thinks his life is so complex.
Grey is his colour, and grey is his being.
People walk by without him seeing.
His mind is saddened day by day,
Hiding his nose amongst the hay.
Can he bear any more pain?
But then, it starts to rain.
Feeling numb and getting wet;
He has still failed to move yet.
As lonely as a statue, standing tall and straight:
Never too early, never too late.
Braying to his shadow, lonely soul;
Young at heart, but, oh, so old.
Someone in the next field neighs;
'Come and be *my* friend,' he says.
Sharing grass, and thoughts as well;
Someone who'll listen and hear him tell
All his troubles and all his fears;
His life story built up over the years.
So now these two aren't lonely:
Patch the horse, and Fred the donkey.

Marcella Meehan (12)
King Edward VI Camp Hill School For Girls, Kings Heath

The Elegant Rose

The elegant rose
Looks lonely in the vase
But looks lovely from afar
Feels like it's put behind bars
Waiting for a couple to come in a car.

The elegant rose
There in such a pose
Acting like a love doze
Beginning to wonder where it will go
Maybe it will be put by someone's nose.

The elegant rose
A sign of love
It works like a clown
Trying not to bring too much harm,
But then sees a woman in alarm.

The elegant rose
Red and bold
Like a trophy made out of gold
Then suddenly picked up to be sold
But with a white rose and knows it's not alone
The elegant red and white rose.

Shivangee Maurya (12)
King Edward VI Camp Hill School For Girls, Kings Heath

Paper - Cinquain

Paper
Bland and inky
Line-ruled, useful, whitish,
Different shapes, many sizes
Paper.

Crystal Griffiths (12)
King Edward VI Camp Hill School For Girls, Kings Heath

And My Spirits Rise

(Inspired by 'And My Heart Scars' by Chief Dan George)

The brightness of the sunshine
The stillness of the moonlight
The sweetness of the air
I hear them all.

The beauty of the sunset
The breaking of the dawn
The waves upon the seashore
I hear them all.

The crying of a newborn deer
The whistling of the breeze
The dew upon the treetops
I hear them all.

The colours of the autumn leaves
The softness of the snow
The sweet rays of the sunshine
I hear them all.

And my spirits rise.

Heather Phoenix (12)
King Edward VI Camp Hill School For Girls, Kings Heath

The Back Of The Bus

They sit at the back of the bus,
Pairs of eyes staring,
Making sure they don't move.
No one cares about the others,
They work hard for nothing,
Ignored, excluded, a group of outsiders,
Rejected by society.
Yet, they sit quietly at the back of the bus.

Nyasha Zvobgo (11)
King Edward VI Camp Hill School For Girls, Kings Heath

The Accidental Poem . . .

Tick . . . tock . . . tick . . . tock . . .
Why do lessons go on . . . and . . . on . . . ?
Sitting at the back,
Looking at the clock . . .

Tick . . . tock . . . tick . . . tock . . .
Why are lessons so monotonous . . . ?
I have to write a poem . . .
But *I can't* think of a subject!

Tick . . . tock . . . tick . . . tock . . .
Looking beyond the person's head in front . . .
Straight . . . through the window . . .
Directly at the trees . . . still . . . no subject . . .

Tick . . . tock . . . tick . . . tock . . .
Looking beyond the trees . . .
Looking beyond the world . . .
Wait . . . yes . . . no . . . *Yes* . . . I have found my answer!

I don't need to write a boring poem . . .
I don't need a subject . . .
I've written one already . . .
And . . . I hope . . . you've just heard it through!

Neha Sandhu (12)
King Edward VI Camp Hill School For Girls, Kings Heath

Artist

I paint:

Snowman in a snowstorm
Black person at night,
Sea against the sky,
Bush in a field of grass,
Chocolate in mud.

Saaira Mushtaq (12)
King Edward VI Camp Hill School For Girls, Kings Heath

Writing Poems

I sit here at my table
Trying to write a poem,
My mind begins to wonder,
What could I do it on?

I look out of the window
Hoping for inspiration,
All I can see are bushes,
In the midst of a dark gloom.

Ideas just pass by me,
While I'm off in a dream world.
I can't seem to concentrate,
For the music is on loud.

If I could just imagine,
One *or* two *good* ideas
I would feel so much better,
As my brain is on stand-by.

Why can I not write poems?
I don't hesitate to ask,
For no one finds it easy,
Except for all of my class!

After all of my effort,
I look down upon my book,
Intending to make a start,
On this impossible task.

It is then that I realise
I have done the gruelling chore,
My poem is together
I will not suffer anymore.

Jo Richards (12)
King Edward VI Camp Hill School For Girls, Kings Heath

Nursery Rhyme

Living in the land of Nursery Rhyme
Time stands still.
Humpty Dumpty sits on a wall and
Falls again.

Though wicked witches lurk in corners with
Wicked stepmums
Snow White still sits and laughs and plays and
Birds fly on.

Skipping, hopscotch, conkers, fun for all,
Light streams,
Though in dark corners, evil lurks,
Here, light streams.

In a shabby book, undecorated,
Solace found,
Escape from the real world, no need to fret,
Solace found.

'Goodbye from Nursery Rhyme Land, drive well!'
Reality
Back to the witches, ghosts and madmen,
Back again.

Emma Crighton (12)
King Edward VI Camp Hill School For Girls, Kings Heath

Get Well Soon

Get well soon Mum,
We're missing you so.
You'd better get home Mum,
Or we're gonna go!

He's driving us nuts, Mum.
He can't even pack
Our basic school lunch, Mum
Or buy a Big Mac!

He's completely nuts, Mum,
His brain's stuffed with cotton.
We finish our clubs Mum,
But we're forgotten!

We hope you get well Mum
And come home real soon.
We don't care what time Mum,
But please before June!

Eleanor Russell (12)
King Edward VI Camp Hill School For Girls, Kings Heath

Ploughing

You pull into the field
Ready to wrestle with the ground
Stones and stubble all around.

You lower the big heavy chasey
With sharp thin blades into the ground.

As you start to drive
The farrows rip up and crumble the ground
All the ground pathetically turns
As the powerful machine rips on through!

Daniel Edwards (14)
Lady Hawkins' School, Kington

My Shed

Open the musty shed
Gather all the tools
The spade, garden fork
And crash them into the wheelbarrow
Cart it over to the ground,
Watch croaking crows flap around the sky
Pick off the caterpillars
Dig a hole for the cabbage
Slot it in its fresh new home
Water its starving roots
Cover its roots with soil
Cart the heavy load to the musty shed
Put the tools back
Drive the cattle to the nice green grass
Take a fork and pluck out the potatoes
Wash them and eat them
You'll never starve again!

Matthew Filbrandt (13)
Lady Hawkins' School, Kington

Peace

Peace lives trapped in boxes
The sound of a perfect world lives there
White mist fills the corners
Smells of clean grass fills it
In the middle lives a big tent
Sounds of laughter and singing fill the air
Something tries to escape but is caught
It's a green and red snake
What would happen if it went?
It would save the world.

Olivia Coppock (13)
Lady Hawkins' School, Kington

Forgotten

The long-forgotten trailer stands silent in the dumping field,
Dead and uncared for, lost but not gone,
Surrounded by piles of brown, dry clay,
Underneath lays the lambs' bleached bones,
Flanked left and right by old, withered trees.
Inside the rusty left-behind trailer,
A little seed of life still remains,
Minute plants and tiny insects,
Lying peaceful in a bed of moss
Protected for eternity from the perils of weather,
From freezing ice and boiling sun,
Protected by the worn and broken tarpaulin,
One day t'will break,
And reveal to them earth.
The long-forgotten trailer stands silent in the field,
Dead and uncared for, lost but not gone.

Kizmet Nibbs (13)
Lady Hawkins' School, Kington

The Colours Of Art

Our lives are filled with colour from the start,
And red is the love that comes from our hearts.
Blue is the sadness that drips from our eyes,
But black is the evil that makes us tell lies.
Green is the shade of jealousy and rage,
And grey is the hair that comes with old age.
Purple is the mood most misunderstood,
But white is the colour that makes us feel good.

Life is full of meaningful colours,
But especially white.
So hold on to it tight.

Daniel Owens (14)
Lady Hawkins' School, Kington

Stag

Staring arrogantly ahead,
A noble expression rested on his face,
Craggy, sharp antlers spear above him,
Curved into the sky, majestically silent.

Ears pointed,
Rigid eyes
Black slits of concentration,
Piercing the night,
Glinting in the moonlight,
Muscle underneath
Ruddy brown fur
Tensed, bunched for action,
Hooves jet-black
Shimmering with dew,
Sure-footed stable
Unbent, legs pulsing
With sinews.

A gunshot burns through the air
The hollow emptiness
And he swallows
Through the dense grass.
A whispering swish is left
Behind him as he goes.

Jasmine Evans (13)
Lady Hawkins' School, Kington

The Box

What is it?
Fear,
Deception,
As I watch it
The soundless nothing taunts me
Like a bullfighter
Is it just me
Or does the box call for me?
I move closer and closer towards it
Like metal to a magnet,
Until my head stares down on it
As an eagle does to its prey.
I move my hand to open it
Just slightly and as I do that
I see the bright white Tasmanian devil eyes
Staring at me in fearful ways.
The eerie smell of sulphur gush
Rushes me away
But the fact of not knowing
Draws me back in.
I open it some more
And somehow I see hands
Capturing me to come in.
The moans and groans of a life sentence
I push the box away
And curl up in the corner,
Wondering.

George Watson (13)
Lady Hawkins' School, Kington

Extinction

I found a box
A dusty box
I held it to my ear
I heard screams
The crackling of a fire
The thud of things hitting the floor
Dying
I opened it slightly
I saw an old dirty bone
The smell of old dirt comes out
The smell of an old room
I opened it a touch more.
The box is bigger on the inside than on the out
I saw a selection of bones
Sitting on a layer of soil
I heard more . . . the sound of crunching bones
Breaking bones
A puff of dust tried to escape
So I slammed the lid shut quickly
If it had escaped into the world
People would have died
For the fear of dying!
Extinction!
So I threw the box to the ground
And jumped on it, crushing the contents.
Then I buried it so none of the contents could escape.

Sophie Jones (13)
Lady Hawkins' School, Kington

Am I In Love?

Just five more minutes to go,
Just five more minutes.
What am I waiting for?
I am waiting to see him,
Or just to get outside?
Will he be happy to see me?
I've got to get ready.

Oh my God, look at me,
I look like I've been electrocuted!
What do I do?
It's too late, the bell's gone.
I walk out slowly, hoping not to see him.
But I want to see him.

This is bad, I can't be in love, I'm not in love
I'm too young, or am I?
He's seen me, he waves.
What do I do?
Do I wave, do I smile, do I ignore him?
I wave. Oh no what have I done?
He's coming towards me, he's coming towards me.

'Will you go out with me?'
'Um, ummm,' who says 'um' when they're in love?
Yes! I'm so happy!
I am in love!

Kelly Owen (14)
Lady Hawkins' School, Kington

Bottled Deception

Who will I find tonight when I return?
I trudge the gravel,
It shudders and cracks beneath my feet.

I see her
With a sway to her stance
One I know too well
Tonight I'll get the it;
The shell.

A creature pushed too far
Depression, but,
No, I shan't deceive myself,
I know too well that consoling lie.

One, I have heard and tell still,
In answer too,
My brother's pitying query,
But why.

I face her, smiling,
Inside me screams, protesting,
Affronted at this façade I bare
To all
My deception.

My turn to take control
Through the house I hunt.
The culprit stands in kingly finery,
The crystal-cut decanter,
The fuel of all deception.

Kathryn McKenna (15)
Lady Hawkins' School, Kington

Guilt Trip

Sitting in the drama unit with tension staring at me,
Is it nearly over?
Uneasy, dramatic feelings bouncing off the walls,
Nervous sweat dripping down my back.
All I want is to escape.
Bitter looks signify anger but the anxiety is easing off.
Subsequently it starts to stop.
It ends and unsteady hugs of farewell show freedom.
I slump in the back seat of the car,
Then the guilt trip starts.

We set off: tense speech turns to anger then
To tears, brain begins to swell with thoughts,
The first neon town, is it over now?
A roundabout, a way out?
But paths are chosen and we speed on to a service station, so static.
A break, a kink in the chain
This chain of feeling.
But it is only another lock,
That holds the shackle fast and increases the pain.

So we set off again, on through the desolate dark, past trees
A forest of emotion.
And houses twinkling with innocence, and the dark
Featureless figures in front, rack me and my conscience,
And the neon lights twinkle out frustration.
Another junction, another apology,
It is best to keep quiet and stare through the window
At the hills and stars as high as my emotions,
The road finally ending
The car slows,
Reverses in the drive, of home.

But the guilt trip is not over yet.

Piran Treen (15)
Lady Hawkins' School, Kington

The Art Of The Word

The pen that flows gracefully
Across an illuminated page,
The black tattoos stain the pure white - like warpaint on tender skin,
Thoughtful description,
On delicate curves,
Twisting, inscribing, racing and leaping,
Dancing on white ice,
It penetrates high councils of democracy,
The blood of our forefathers - in ink honoured,
Basis of intelligent foundations,
Axis of conversation,
Scripted and written in the stone,
Its letters caress the blank space - like blossoming dove feathers
Hovering on the breeze,
Those lines crowned with punctuated blooms,
Sentences crafted by wordsmiths of old,
The scented fragrance of knowledge,
A burning desire and intense pursuit flamboyantly displayed
                                          on the page,

All inspired by a word.

Matthew Lampitt (13)
Lady Hawkins' School, Kington

Tina

Tina's hidden grey
Was as white as snow.

Any harm she brought,
Was sorrowful.

Her mane and tail flowed,
With sheer innocence.

Her stance was powerful
But kind.

The Arab in her made
Her tail flow.

In each step she took
The lightness shone through.

When she trotted with grace,
She showed you affection.

Her expressive canter
Told us she could have won a million rosettes.

Her head collar still lies,
In a drawer of memories.

Joanne Allford (13)
Lady Hawkins' School, Kington

Why

Peace lives in this box.
Shouts, gunfire, screams, blood,
Ceased by a single voice.
One silhouette stands alone
Putrid blood fouls the stagnant air.
Two armies parted by one soul.
One question,
Why?
Fear, death, anger, battling to escape.
To set them free,
To save mankind,
Throw the lid wide,
Let them fly,
Into uncertainty,
Out of this world
To leave Earth in peace.
That one voice,
The harbinger of peace
The voice of the inner child.

Ellen Baines (13)
Lady Hawkins' School, Kington

On Walking In A Field Of Sheep

Is this how it feels to be a god?
Some vengeful thing walking in the fog;
They gather in the hole I leave behind.
Will they remember me, do you think,
Or am I just the same tall man hung in new wools?

The aproned midwife drains his flask;
Through the February winds the bleating drifts:
He wrestles in the messy birth with some new life.
April calls the fleecy man with the obscene tattoo;
His beard is scratchy as he conducts the blades
And from the baptised cuttings he makes a robe;
In the night the man in the leather top
Takes the lamb he is owed; his rightful sacrifice.

When the grass is dying, will you pray to me?
I cannot birth your young, or create or destroy;
I serve no purpose but to stumble through the fog
And remind you of the strangest things.

James Gardiner (18)
Lady Hawkins' School, Kington

The Whistle

Waiting for the whistle, Selhurst Park is so tense
Palace drawing with Man U,
United attack is their best defence.
From Palace's Andrew Johnson
Blasting the ball into the back of the net
That's most fans' nightmare
Losing to a relegation side.
Five mins added for injury time,
Palace fans all moan.
Man U are throwing everything at Palace
But still nothing's happened
Gabor Kiraly saves a point-blank range shot from
Wayne Rooney
Palace are hanging on . . .
The final whistle is blown
Selhurst Park erupts with joy and relief
That Palace have drawn with Man U.

Dominic Barnes (14)
Lady Hawkins' School, Kington

Make Poverty History!

There's a war we must fight
Not a war with guns
Not a war with men
But a war against death
A war against Aids
A war against hunger
A war against thirst
A war against poverty
Only we have the power
To make poverty go away
So it's time to take a stand
It's time to make poverty history.

Hannah Foxon (13)
Littleover Community School, Derby

Charity

What is charity?
A sympathetic cause to give
Money, clothes, quilts and shoes
For those who can't buy them themselves
Those who don't even have homes.

Why do we give?
Because we feel sorrow for the homeless
Who live on the streets; in gutters, in shelters,
Those who could die any time soon.

When will this end?
Probably never.
There will always be those
With no food, no clothes, no homes,
No lives!

Katie Bradford (13)
Littleover Community School, Derby

Mother's Day Poem

I love you Mum
You are the best
You comfort me
When I rest
We sometimes fall out
But I don't mean what I say
We always make up
The very next day
I love you Mum
Because you see
I have you Mum
And you have me.

Happy Mother's Day.

Laura Hewitson (13)
Littleover Community School, Derby

The Music

Who would have thought?
Notes, mere vibrations, circling through the air
Air circulating, moving the sounds to our ears
The music catching us in its peaceful grasp
Floating us around like a feather.

Then off
A flick,
A new track to play
The noisy hum of the frantic beat
Electricity, turning into the sound that we hear
Twisting us
Turning us
Rocking our soul.

Again, a change
New games to play
And now, the sound of a voice
The singing, winding into our brain
A worm, catching a tune
The sound swings, making us sing
A track too repetitive to lose.

Now it's left, another beat
Tap-tap-tapping on a drum
Vibrations again, moving the floor
The quick, sharp voice, bouncing around
A rapping tune, dancing through the air
Quickening the route to our ears
The voice so quick, it's like a cat
Thundering its feet on the ground

The tunes surround us, circle us, grope us
A song that anyone can hear
Find your mood, find a song
Whatever you want to feel
The music takes us, a story far away
We can let go, relax
What would we do without these blissful tunes?
They let us out of our bottled trap.

Jennifer Unwin (13)
Littleover Community School, Derby

Perfect World

I open my eyes:
And what do I see?
A world full of flowers, sunshine and trees,
The people live in peace:
Of mind and soul,
The world has no poor,
And no one asking for more.
A world that has not shed a tear,
For someone so dear,
A friend, or a person in need,
That needed our help,
That wasn't so dear.

And as I look back today,
Where did it all go so wrong?
For that world that was perfect,
Wasn't perfect for long!
The crying, the dying,
The starvation, the desecration,
The pollution, no solution.
But the thing I hate most,
There wasn't a single person that cared!
For that perfect world.

So I ask myself:
And why is it so?
Then I remember:
It's because of people,
Like you and like me,
That become tempted,
With jealousy,
Big-headedness, and wanting more,
The grief and the anger taking control.

So all the dying and killing;
What's it all for?
This world that used to be perfect,
But it's not anymore.

Sarah Taylor (13)
Littleover Community School, Derby

Hate

I live in this world of hate
People discriminate,
Terrorism, bombs, murders, assassinations
Take what the presidents say
Let them lead the way
To war and hatred
Let them do whatever they say
Let them lead us
To this future, this terrible fate.

We will argue about it
We will protest about it
Say it loud and we will shout it out
We care about it!

Bombs, murders, killing each other
All they do – presidents –
Have they no other
Motive or plan to get
Their country to be one?
A democracy, a nation,
A union in which
All races get along.
Where there's no murder
No bombs
Or assassinations
To kill each other in this world.
This world of hate.

Harkiran Sagoo (14)
Littleover Community School, Derby

The UK!

Six bombs in one day,
People dead or alive,
People stop to pray,
Others deprive,
This is the UK!

Today,
Terrorists attack!
Affecting innocent and harmless people,
But we will fight back!
As we are the UK's people!
This is the UK!

Today,
We take time to remember,
Women and men,
Just like the 11th of September,
We hope this does not happen again,
This is the UK!

Today,
My birthday goes down in history,
9/11!
But who is to blame? That my friend remains a mystery,
Let us hope those innocent that died go to Heaven,
This is the one and only UK!

Anita Ghei (13)
Littleover Community School, Derby

A Wonderful World?

Bung up the bunghole on the barrel of terrorists,
Stop them getting out, but not short term,
Lock them in,
Lock them in for life.
Think of the lives that could have been spared,
What if one was yours?
Lock them in,
Lock them in for life.
Imagine a walk in the park,
Ended in a tunnel with a bright light at the end,
Lock them in,
Lock them in for life.
Ponder upon the families that have been destroyed,
Think of the tears that could have been saved,
Lock them in,
Lock them in for life.
Stop, full stop.

Matthew Sheffield (13)
Littleover Community School, Derby

Depths Of Our Love

My love flows deeper than you'll ever know
As though the hole in the ozone layer melted the pole
It's lasting like the moon in the sky, as though it was established
before our time
Like the roots of a tree, strong as can be
Keeps us grounded, meanwhile our branches grow free
It's as though the sun stopped shining and there you were,
Guiding limitless love.
No need to stop and ponder the future
Cos there you were like fate.
The key, my heart, the gate.
So be my valentine as our hearts entwine,
Your destiny's mine, the past erased time.

Keshia Russell (12)
Lordswood Girls' School, Harborne

I Wanna Be Yours

(Inspired by 'I Wanna Be Yours' by John Cooper Clarke)

Let me be your window
To keep you locked up tight
Let me be your pillow
To rest your head at night
If you like your dishes clean
Let me be your dish-washing machine
Whatever you need,
I wanna be yours.

Let me be your curtains
When you need privacy
Let me be your dream car
So you can ride with me
Let me be your outdoor flowers
I will grow each day for hours
You've got the power
I wanna be yours.

Let me be your armchair
For those restless working days
Let me be your bus fare
So you can go away
Let me be your shining star
Guiding you to near and far
Far as the furthest shining star
That's how far is the furthest star
Far, far, far, far, far, far, far,
I don't wanna be his
I wanna be yours.

Eleanor Mason (12)
Lordswood Girls' School, Harborne

I Wanna Be Yours

(Inspired by 'I Wanna Be Yours' by John Cooper Clarke)

Let me be your cooking maid
I'll never let you down
Let me by your 'A' Level grades
You'll never have to frown
If you like to walk for miles
Let me be your walking styles
I do smile
I wanna be yours.

Let me be your protecting shell
You'll never face bad
Let me be your friendly pal
You'll never feel so bad
Let me be your machine that grinds
Whatever you need I will find
I don't mind
I wanna be yours.

Let me be your toothbrush
Keeping those teeth clean
Let me be your machine that crushes
Please don't be mean.
Let me be in your emotions
Loving you all the time
Loving you with hard devotion
Hard as the hard
Dried lotion
That's how hard is my emotion
Hardy, hardy, hardy, hardy de hard
I don't want to be his
I wanna be yours,
I wanna be yours.

Nosheen Tabassum (12)
Lordswood Girls' School, Harborne

Let Me Be Yours

(Inspired by 'I Wanna Be Yours' by John Cooper Clarke)

Let me be your household lamp,
Giving you some light,
Let me be your postage stamp,
Colourful, bold and bright.
If you like to study the stars,
Let me be the planet Mars,
So you can see me from afar
I wanna be yours.

Let me be your personal planner,
Fill in all your dates,
Let me be your welcome home banner,
I'll invite all your mates,
Let me be your heart's desire,
Love as hot as burning fire,
Believe in me I'm not a liar,
I wanna be yours.

Let me be your beautiful sun,
Wake you up each day,
Let me be your bundle of fun,
Happiness all through May.
Let me be your cuddly cat,
Hold me tight,
Place me on my mat
Don't mind my weight,
I know I'm quite fat.
I'm watching you, you're beautifully sat,
Love is our fate,
I hope it lasts,
Time with you goes so fast!

Sunaina Deol (12)
Lordswood Girls' School, Harborne

I Wanna Be Yours

(Inspired by 'I Wanna Be Yours' by John Cooper Clarke)

Let me be your leaf,
Where cold winter will be,
Let me be your sunshine,
Where you can only be mine,
If you like your drink cold,
Meet me at the North Pole,
Let me be your woolly clothes
Keep you nice and warm at night,
I don't wannabe his,
I wanna be yours.

Let me be your dairy,
Tell me what you want,
Let me be your biro,
Write whatever you want,
Let me be your duvet,
Keep you warm at night,
I don't wanna be his,
I wanna be yours.

Divya Rani (12)
Lordswood Girls' School, Harborne

I Wanna Be Yours

(Inspired by 'I Wanna Be Yours' by John Cooper Clarke)

Let me be your comfy bed
So you can hold tight
Let me be your star
So I can shimmer in the night
If you like cream let me
Be the cream on your hot chocolate
All I want is to be yours
I wanna be yours!

Let me be your car
I will ride you through the night
Let me be your sunshine
I will brighten up your day.
Let me be your water fountain
When you need a drink
Please let me be yours, that's all I ask
I wanna be yours!

Elizabeth Sinton (11)
Lordswood Girls' School, Harborne

I Wanna Be Yours Forever And Always

(Inspired by 'I Wanna Be Yours' by John Cooper Clarke)

Let me be your amplifier
Playing your music day and night
Let me be your gas fire
Keeping the room warm and bright
If you like your cakes hot
Let me be the cherry on top
I'm not asking for a lot
I wanna be yours.

Let me be our candyfloss
Lush, sweet and pink
Let me be your lipgloss
Shimmering like an ice rink
Let me be your sunlight
Shielding you from rain
I will never bring you pain
I wanna be yours.

Let me be your Red Bull
Energetic, bubbly and bright
Let me be your cotton wool
Keeping you warm all night
Let me be your cosy socks
Keeping your toes warm inside
Warm as the warmest smock
Warm, warm, warm, warm, warm,
That's how warm is my devotion
I don't wanna be his
I wanna be yours.

Candice Edwards (12)
Lordswood Girls' School, Harborne

I Wanna Be Yours

(Inspired by 'I Wanna Be Yours' by John Cooper Clarke)

Let me be your toothbrush
Your teeth will stay sparkly, shiny clean
Let me be your cushion dust
For those lovely sleepy dreams
If you like your delicious rice
Let me be your pot of spice
I don't wanna be his
I wanna be yours.

Let me be your teddy bear
With tasty chocolate mints
Let me be your setting lotion
For your soft skin
Let me be your snack
Tied in a sack
If it's heavy I'll carry it on my back
I wanna be yours.

Let me be your shiny shoes
For miserable rainy days
Let me be your crew ship
When you want to sail away
Let me be your red rose
For sweet smelling scent
With deep, deep emotions
Really, really deep
As deep as the deep devotion
And beautiful potion
Deep - deep - de - deep - deep
I don't wanna be his
I wanna be yours.

Sahila Khanum (12)
Lordswood Girls' School, Harborne

I Wanna Be Yours!

(Inspired by 'I Wanna Be Yours' by John Cooper Clarke)

Let me be your Scoubidous,
To put on your keyrings
Let me be your Winnie the Pooh
To snuggle up with you in bed,
If you like your bag packed,
Let me be your rucksack,
To put on your back,
I wanna be yours.

Let me be your summer hat,
To put on your head,
Let me be your furry cat,
To stay with you in bed,
Let me be your teddy bear,
I'll go with you anywhere,
I wanna be yours.

Let me be your comfy chair,
I will never spare
Let me be your Care Bear
So you can style my furry hair,
Let me be your sunshine,
I'll take you anywhere,
And you'll always be mine,
I'll always be there for you
When you're not fine
I'll take you away to dine,
You'll be my only love too,
I don't want to be his,
I wanna be yours.

Monica Chirrimar (12)
Lordswood Girls' School, Harborne

I Wanna Be Yours

(Inspired by 'I Wanna Be Yours' by John Cooper Clarke)

Let me be your helicopter
I'll fly you anywhere
Let me be your sweet lobster
I will take good care
If you like a laugh
Let me be your guide or map
I can also do a very good rap.

Let me be your tasty mint
So your breath will never stink
Let me be your clean shiny sink
So you can have a drink
Let me be your cooking book
So that you can learn to cook
And I can learn and look.

Let me be your zooming car
Zooming round like a star
Let me be your dress that's pink
Please don't throw me in the bin
Let me be your suncream lotion
To make your skin so smooth
With deep devotion
Deep as the Atlantic ocean,
That's how deep is my emotion
Please come back with all your emotion,
You call the shots
I wanna be yours.

Gaganjit Sandhu (12)
Lordswood Girls' School, Harborne

The Art Lesson

A splat of pink and a flick of blue,
And maybe even some purple too,
Paints are flying everywhere,
Some on my work, but a lot in my hair.

Clean my paintbrush in the water below,
I'm speeding through it, I hate going slow,
Like a conductor waving his arms around,
Getting so sucked into artistry, I could have drowned.

Back and forth, left and right,
Every direction there is in sight!
My uniform is covered from head to toe,
With the wonderful colours that seem to glow.

I stop and stand back to see what I've done,
It looks complete, but I've only just begun.
I signed my work and raised my hand,
The teacher came over and said 'That's grand.'

Jillian Alger (13)
Lordswood Girls' School, Harborne

I Wanna Be Yours!

(Inspired by 'I Wanna Be Yours' by John Cooper Clarke)

I wanna be yours!
Let me be your glittering toothbrush
To keep your teeth shining clean
Let me be your lipgloss lush
To make your lips look keen
If you like your toothpaste taste
Let me be your toothpaste taste
I'm always on your case
I wanna be yours.

Let me be all the pleasures prove
To keep our marriage alive.
Let me be your first love
Because I love you very much alive
All I wanna say is I don't want to be his
I wanna be yours.

Simerpreet Sanghera (12)
Lordswood Girls' School, Harborne

I Wanna Be Yours

(Inspired by 'I Wanna Be Yours' by John Cooper Clarke)

Let me be your pillow
That you cuddle up at night
Let me be your limo
And I'll drive you through the light
If you like your milkshake pink
Let me be your favourite drink
But please don't pour me down the sink
I wanna be yours.

Let me be your cuddly bear
That you take with you everywhere
Let me be our sweet bowl
That you will never share
Let me be your morning sun
That will melt your lovely creamy bun
That you shall take and run.

Let me be your birthday cake
Full of twinkling lights
Let me be your gorgeous lake
Where you can fly some kites
Let me be your umbrella protecting you from rain
To keep you warm
To keep you dry
With deep devotion
Deep as the Atlantic ocean
That's how deep is my emotion
Deep, deep, deep, deep de deep
I don't wanna be his
I wanna be yours!

Munira Muflehi (11)
Lordswood Girls' School, Harborne

Stand

I stand and stare
This world is not bare,
Filled with trees and bees
Cats and dogs,
Toads and frogs!

I stand and stare
This world is not bare,
Shoppers shopping,
Swimmers swimming,
And me writing.

I stand and stare,
This world is not bare,
It makes me sad,
Because it's bad
This world's not bare,
I know, I stood and stared!

Jasdeep Kandola (12)
Lordswood Girls' School, Harborne

Love

I love the way you look at me
I love the way you smile softly
I love the way you walk and talk.

You're my hero holding me tight,
When I look at you, I see nothing else in sight.

I see you in my dreams later in life
That you will be my hubby and I'll be your wife.

At the end of this tunnel there is a bright light,
'Cause I believe in love at first sight.

I love you!

Becky Shirley (13)
Moseley Park School, Bilston

London Rocked By Terror Attacks

London was nice and calm; people were smiling through the town.
There suddenly appeared to be a big *bang!*
People were screaming
Their smiles were wiped off their faces,
It was all a big disgrace.
London rocked by terror attacks.

People's happiness turned into sadness,
People crying, injured or dead,
Trying to fix their lives back together.
Residents of London were shocked as hell,
They left the place without a doubt.
London rocked by terror attacks.

London turned into a fright,
The city was out of light.
Liveliness died,
Families were very unsatisfied.
People cried on Thursday morning at 9.45.
London rocked by terror attacks.

London was great, London was interesting,
But somebody ruined the beautiful sights.
There were four explosions,
One on a bus and three at Kings Cross train station.
Fifty-three are known to be dead.
Seven hundred are injured and still more to be found.
London rocked by terror attacks,
London rocked by terror attacks.

Leena Patel (13)
Moseley Park School, Bilston

London

Thursday morning came along,
The streets of London were busy,
Roads were jammed, footpaths crowded,
Buses, trains and tubes were packed
But everyone was happy,
No one had the slightest idea of the terror that awaited.

In the blink of an eye everything changed,
The people of London became outraged.
Bombs tore the city apart,
As the working day was about to start.
Innocent lives were lost.

After the terror came an eerie silence,
Disbelief and sorrow followed.
People searched for loved ones in vain,
Hoping they would see them again.

Lee Potts (13)
Moseley Park School, Bilston

Relationships

We fell out yesterday and I don't know why,
It hurt me so much that it made me cry.
Why did the conversation change so much,
What I wouldn't give now to feel your touch.

Mad, moody, but miserable, I sit here and wait,
Thinking that you are my perfect soulmate.
I want to see you and know how you feel,
And for you to say that it's no big deal.

I spoke to you today and all was OK,
All the things I'd said had been forgotten through the day.
I now don't feel any more sorrow,
I'm happy that it's nine months tomorrow!

Samantha Pritchard (15)
Moseley Park School, Bilston

RIP

RIP to all the people that died.
Your families have lost their joy and pride.
Wishing you had survived
You didn't deserve to die.
All this tragedy, *why?*
Over fifty lives were taken,
Why were they forsaken?
Why can't people see that all they're causing
Is pain and misery.

We all had a two minute silence
For all the people that have gone
All down to the London bomb.

RIP.

Whitney Barton (12)
Moseley Park School, Bilston

London Is Dead

Mass destruction all over the world,
Children up in corners curled.
Grenades and rockets everywhere,
People hiding anywhere.

Planes up in the sky,
People don't know why.
How did they get there?
People are unaware.

People looking everywhere,
Everybody stressed and losing their hair.
Debris blasting into cars behind,
People dying inside.

Stephen Bayliss (13)
Moseley Park School, Bilston

London Bombing

At 9.42
The first bomb blew,
The second was due,
Then it went too,
Spreading terror and sorrow through the town
But we swore so well, we wouldn't go down.

Trees burning
Trains overturning
The fate we are learning
The love we are yearning,
Oh, London's burning.

We will fight
Day and night
To prevent fright
And keep terror out of sight.

Natalie Wolverson (13)
Moseley Park School, Bilston

London Bombing

L ondon has been bombed - what a terrible fate
O bstacles are overcome
N oises are heard, sirens and screaming
D estroyed and damaged
O bliteration has happened
N ow everything's gone, people and family
But now you know, it's only just begun.

Katherine Owen (13)
Moseley Park School, Bilston

London Bombs!

Booms and bangs are all I can hear,
I flip my car into first gear.
When I arrive, nobody's around,
No one speaks or moves
No matter where I go,
No one makes a sound.

It seems that World War 3 has taken place,
So our fate is war – we shall face.
The bombing battle has now been triggered,
For we are strong, as they've figured.

A normal day gone wrong,
Our families hearts beating strong,
Some people close to losing their life,
It could have been your husband, it could've been your wife.
Shouting and screaming for all the lives that are lost,
From the evil happenings, our lives have cost.

We're marching through this eerie silence,
After lots and lots of horrible violence.
Our fellow soldiers are still killing,
But none of us can hear a single thing.

Lauren Field (13)
Moseley Park School, Bilston

Highbury

H ome of Arsenal FC's greatest games
 I t's lasted for over one hundred years
G lorified championship moments it has witnessed
H igh in the heart of London it stands
B uried with history it will be in 2006
U nited with the Premiership title it might never be.
R ed and white paint it wears
Y our chants will always be welcome there.

Raja Clair (15)
Moseley Park School, Bilston

Terrorists' War

In all wars there is slaughter
If I was you, I'd lock up your daughter
Hatred is shown
Objects are thrown
Screaming is heard in the street
While a bomb is planted under a bus seat.

Normal day, travelling to work
Looking forward to the coffee perc
They got on the bus
Making a big fuss
Bang! Bang! Some black out
While the rest begin to shout.

Terrorists begin to flee the town
While forensics go underground
Dead bodies carpeting the floor
Police know it's a bomb for sure.

My children were only seven
Now they're dead, they've gone to Heaven.
I suppose I'm lucky to be alive,
But sometimes I wonder why I survived.

Vinod Birdi (13) & Tia Rafferty (13)
Moseley Park School, Bilston

School's Out

S chool's out, we get a break
C hildren running for the gate
H olidays have come at last
O h my God, we'll have a blast
O ur year has gone once again
L ife's going down the drain.

O ut again and feeling fine
U p to no good, parents draw the line
T ime has gone so fast, now it's time to get back in class!

Kayleigh Evans (13)
Moseley Park School, Bilston

I Am

I am the life in the flower in your vase,
I am the food you eat giving you energy,
I am the sun giving light to the world,
I am the rain bouncing off your face,
I am the wood of the chair you sit on,
I am inside of you, a memory in your mind.
I am with you always, watching you
So don't feel sad.
I am always by your side, smiling.

I am the seed that creates new life,
I am the tree at the bottom of your garden,
I am the shoes you put upon your feet,
I am the blanket you wrap around you,
I am the water you drink,
I am the bed you lay on.
I am with you always, watching you
So don't feel sad
I am always by your side, smiling.

I am the guitar you play,
I am the cereal box on the kitchen table,
I am the wind howling through the air,
I am the leaves on the ground,
I am the stars above in the midnight sky,
I am your pet dog you love so dearly,
I am with you always, watching you.
So don't feel sad,
I am always by your side, smiling.

Jade Davis (15)
Moseley Park School, Bilston

People As Statistics!

You don't know me,
I'm another number on a list.
But you don't care,
You don't know I even exist.
I am a teenage suicide,
Who never knew their worth.
I'm another starving baby,
An accident at birth.
I'm a victim of domestic violence,
Who nobody will listen to.
I'm the beggar on the street corner,
But what can I do?
I'm a child without a school,
Because no one will do a good deed.
I'm a poor worker with no money,
But five children to feed.
I'm a child without a family,
So I'll get thrown into care.
I'm the starving unemployed,
I am everywhere!
I am an old lady,
Cold and dying in the snow.
But you have a home,
So what would you know?
I could be anyone.
Anyone that I wanted to.
I could be closer than you think.
I am standing next to you.
I am another number on a list.
Now you know I do exist.

Hayley Bate   (15)
Moseley Park School, Bilston

West Bromwich Albion FC

W onderful football for the full ninety minutes
E xcellent players giving it their best
S coring goals from all over the pitch
T ension builds as the final minutes draw near.

B oing, boing baggies
R oaming around, jumping up and down –
O n the ground
M oaning as the goals are let in
W ondering what's happening
 I s this the best we can play?
C heer them on to get them started
H ere it all happens, at the Hawthorns.

A nger as the whistle is blown
L osing again, is this the end?
B oing boing baggies
 I nteraction is what it needed!
O n the pitch it all has changed
N ow we are Premier League once again!

Chris Bray (15)
Moseley Park School, Bilston

London Bombing

London, London, sweet and sound
Suddenly a bomb shakes the ground
Making everything seem so loud
All the evil spreads around.

Body parts are flying
While others are dying
People moaning, people crying

A week ago, it was all so bright
Then four people turned out the light.

Jagdeep Sandhu (13)
Moseley Park School, Bilston

Friends

Friends last forever
Roaming around the streets
Independent we call ourselves
Everyone lives their own life.

Never ending the fun
With many stories to tell
Taking a detour to find a new way home
Sounds of laughter fill the air!

Forever together, having a laugh
And comforting friends when they're down.
Kicking up a fuss when protecting your closest,
Even helping them right their wrongs.

Always there for a shoulder to cry on
Keeping your friends close to you
Making sure you never let them go
As a friend as close as this, would never dream of letting you go!

Rebekah O'Neil (15)
Moseley Park School, Bilston

Untitled

I tried to be perfect,
It just wasn't worth it.
You didn't believe a word that I said.
It would have been so easy,
But you didn't believe me.
And now that it's over, so long and goodbye,
I hate that you blame me, I really did try,
I know it still hurts but it can't get much worse,
Now that you've left me behind.
I've said I'm sorry,
What else can I say?
It didn't have to be this way.
So long and goodbye,
I hate that you blame me, I really did try.

Siobhan Codner (15)
Moseley Park School, Bilston

Destruction

In this world of technology and electric
Where people's thoughts are all diseased and septic
Some believe what is wrong is right
Some believe what is right is wrong
Who are we to decide and put up a fight?
All we can do is join in and sing the song.

The people of this Earth, go to work and carry on like a normal day
Little do they know they will lose their life and be a stray
The men who cause blasts and shed blood
The tears of loved ones that face a flash flood.

It's OK, it's alright
It's something that those men have forced to ignite
We will not back down
We will not frown
All it will become is a tit for tat plea
I hit you and then you hit me.

Monica Patel (17)
Moseley Park School, Bilston

Forbidden Young Love

Wouldn't life be so much better if we could express our love again?
I thought you loved me but how can that be?
You just weren't meant for me,
I refer to you as a dream come true,
But we can't start anew,
You have surrounded me in happiness,
But when I found you, you were my greatest weakness,
You said, 'Our love will take us everywhere,'
But now it is getting us nowhere,
Why did you have to hurt me?
Why couldn't you just let it be?
'If only,' that is all I say,
You may come back another day.

Samantha Turner (17)
Moseley Park School, Bilston

Falling Into Death

Walking down a lonely lane,
Nobody in sight.
Past thatched cottages, dressed with flowers,
But the flowers are dead!
Withered and black.
Death oozing out of the cracks of windows and doors,
Infecting everything, everyone around.
Dead animals lying rigid on the path,
Their eyes still open, looking startled.
What are they scared of?

My eyes dart everywhere,
Looking for any sign of movement
The dead flowers rustling in the slight breeze,
Making the atmosphere even more eerie.
A rattling breath, slowly inhaling and exhaling.
I can feel all of my life slowly draining away
I cannot physically or emotionally move,
Frozen to the spot.
Death oozing into my mouth, slowly taking my body,
Falling into death.

Natalie Sheargold (15)
Moseley Park School, Bilston

Forest No More (Or The Chainsaw Attacks)

Stretching upwards towards the warm glow,
Onwards, upwards, constant, slow.
Gnarled brown fingers reach up high,
Anchored old man, the time is nigh.
Roaring, growling, aggressive beast,
Moves in to attack, only to cease,
When death has swept over and taken this life,
After years of battles and storms and strife.

Catherine Holmes (16)
Moseley Park School, Bilston

Life, Happiness and Cynicism

Never expect gratitude to come to you,
Because people aren't grateful for what you do,
People never stop to think, saying 'thank you' would be nice,
Oh no, never, these people never stop to think twice,
But then again, I shouldn't moan,
For it is human nature and that can be bad to the bone.
People are thinking of themselves every minute of the day,
No matter what they hear you say,
But this is the price we have to pay,
For people have no morals in the world today,
Our life is what our thoughts make it,
And we should take care what we do just a little bit,
There is no time to think of life wasting away,
We should take life easy, just day by day,
Don't let people bring you down,
Slap on a big, broad smile and wipe away the frown,
Let's not waste a minute thinking of people we don't like,
And if they criticise us let's just say 'On your bike,'
You'll feel better with a smile on your face,
Whatever the time or wherever the place,
You'll gain a positive upsurge from deep inside of you,
And it will diminish those feelings of being sad and blue,
So let's always look on the bright side of life,
So that we don't end up in stress and strife,
Let's do what we do and do it the best,
And all spend some time to joke and jest,
Let's dish out love, care and concern every night,
And let's go through life trying to do most things right.

Katie Dudwell (15)
Moseley Park School, Bilston

Love Is Deep And Meaningful

Love is deep and meaningful.
Yet, our love cannot be.
The way it has turned out is so hurtful,
It really hurt me.
I thought you were special and that we would last a long time,
But now I realise that you will never be mine!
You're living your life without me,
While I lie crying, thinking of you and me.
You were so close for a time,
But now you are so far away, I can't see your face.
I remember the time when you were mine,
But now love has forgotten this lonely place.
Every time I see you or talk to you,
The pain is unbearable.
I know I should start anew.
Now that I see you are moving on, it's so unimaginable.
Many nights I stayed up just to talk to you,
I thought you felt the same,
But now I know that it was just to suit you.
I lie awake at night trying to tame the tears that you made.

Many years have passed since that sad July day,
The day you took your love away,
I wonder where you are now?
It's been so long, so much has happened
Since that final row.
Much has been said, seen and done.
But how can I say that in the end we both won?
We both started our lives separately,
But I still want you desperately.
I hope that you love and are loved,
I hope that you are happy and live forever with your beloved.
I also hope that one day, in this life or the next,
That we can see each other once again,
If I could, I would live my life with you once more.

Samantha Baker (17)
Moseley Park School, Bilston

Sad, Lonely, Pathetic Girl

Looking in the mirror
But there's nothing there to see
Just a sad, lonely, pathetic girl
How sad is that, that girl is me.

Cutting at her wrists now
The blood pouring out
Can't anybody help this girl?
Give her something to feel special about.

Suddenly there's a knock at the door
Her true love comes rushing in
Their eyes meet at the edge of death
Nothing could come between the feelings they had within

Rushing to the hospital
Around the sirens go
Is it too late to save this girl now?
It's too early yet to know

Lying in a hospital bed now
He sits there and stares
Who knows who this girl is and why he saved her?
But then again, who cares?

Three years later
Happily wed they are
With a house, a dog and three kids
And a big red car.

The girl is finally happy at last
That sad, lonely, pathetic girl is a thing of the past.

Jade Reynolds (15)
Moseley Park School, Bilston

Mankind's Failures

The human rights, they called them so,
Applied to all mankind.
Yet mankind now have fallen so low,
No more than ignorance you'll find.

How is it that men upon the moon can walk?
Of life's petty obstacles they'll talk,
Yet the world's own contents we cannot feed,
Dismissed as beautiful gardens' weed!

Harken now to the objective,
Just to put things in perspective,
You cannot bite the hand that feeds,
Hence, we must tend one to another's needs.
To treat others as you would have them treat you,
Is that so hard for mankind to do?

Heather Rogers (17)
Moseley Park School, Bilston

My Escape

Music is life, escape from reality.
When feeling lonely music helps me through
For secrets of my life, music is the key.
It makes me happy when I'm feeling blue.
I'm in another world when listening,
I like the sounds, tunes, grace of it all.
Can people see it's a beautiful thing?
It picks me up when I'm about to fall.
Music can help me through times good and bad.
If I could, I would listen all day long.
It makes me smile, it's all I've really had.
I like it all, I don't have a fave song.
It's life, you can either love or hate.
But in these eyes, music is my fate!

Kayleigh Biles (14)
Our Lady & St Chad Catholic School, Wolverhampton

The Seventh Of The Seventh

A raging inferno enveloped the town;
London city is burning down.
Explosions caused by explosive devices,
Within fifty seconds, four more surprises.
Several bombs were detonated that day,
Survivors suffered pain and dismay.
A sea of corpses, a river of blood
Terrorists caused as much pain as they could.
A very large void opened in England's hearts,
For all those who from this life did part.
'We will prevail' revealed a speech from Blair;
As death and devastation conquered the air.
As Britain stands together side by side,
We will not be scared.
We will not hide.

Amy Jones (15)
Our Lady & St Chad Catholic School, Wolverhampton

Racism

Why the hell are people racist to me?
We are all humans just different colours
I mean how the hell are we meant to be?
We don't have to be the same like others.
If we're the same things would be too perfect,
Being different colours is creative
Martin Luther King spoke it was worth it!
But for that he was assassinated!
The great Martin Luther was a brave man
He let out all the emotions he had
He said that he had a dream or a plan
He thought the way the world thought was quite bad.
People in the world should not be racist
Humans are all the same, so just face it!

Cherelle Wright (15)
Our Lady & St Chad Catholic School, Wolverhampton

Moved On

You see I'm there,
But you don't look,
Without a care
My heart you took.

I let you walk all over me,
Not once, but twice before,
Was I too blind to see
That you kept coming back for more?

As time goes by
I look back and think,
At the times you made me cry,
And how much you made me drink.

But now I've moved on,
After all the strife,
Our love has come and gone,
And I've moved on with my life.

Laura Hill (15)
Our Lady & St Chad Catholic School, Wolverhampton

Make Poverty History . . .

Every day is a long, hard battle,
Feeling weak and life can't go on.
All they can see is the bony cattle,
The heat from the sun burned down as it shone,
Waiting for at least a taste of water.
Can't you see these poor people need saving?
Just for a mother to see her daughter,
For a brighter day they are all craving.
Please, will you give them a bit of your love?
A chance to see what it's like to be well,
Would you be OK if your life just fell?
So will you please give up a bit of love,
I think these people have had enough.

Latisha Farrington (15)
Our Lady & St Chad Catholic School, Wolverhampton

Coffee Shop

The two of us sat there,
Reclined in a sofa chair
Sipping on coffee
Chewing on crème patissiere.

We chatted for hours
The time, it was ours
And oh, how it flew by
It was fun, you and I.

When we had finished
The time had diminished
You got up to stand,
You offered your hand.

Together we both talked
Out of the coffee shop we both walked
To go back to the car park
For October, it was quite dark.

Then as we were leaving,
The clouds started heaving,
Lucky we were in your car,
Our journeys home were never far.

As we pulled round the crescent,
In the heat of the moment,
In the light of the fly-by,
You kissed me goodbye.

Samuel Fullwood (15)
Our Lady & St Chad Catholic School, Wolverhampton

Terrorism

Training camps
Hot sun blazing,
Sand blowing, drifting along the sky.
Weapons firing,
Exploding sounds,
Bullets dropping among the sand,
Squinting eyes.

Night fire, all huddled around,
Raising voices, praising God.
Consequences of martyrdom being conferred,
Orders received, conscience beating.

Final hours, time ticking slow,
Watching among the rush of busy foreigners
Heaven and God are near
The suffering of people and my suicide will decide my fate
A freedom fighter of belief, or a coward?
Sweaty palms, conscience racing against my heartbeat.
The time has come, countdown
5 . . . 4 . . . 3 . . . 2 . . . 1
The bomb explodes, praise to my God
Screams fighting for life and my final breath on Earth.

Nitika Punj (15)
Our Lady & St Chad Catholic School, Wolverhampton

Winning Our Match

We all played well in our last rounders match,
Miss Creig and Miss Ellis were watching us,
The ball in the air we all shouted, 'Catch,'
Missing the ball makes us go red and blush.
Alexe is the bowler, she is so good,
Steph is the backstop she's quick off the spot
Sam is the sub but she'd bat if she could
Tandi plays well but she giggles a lot.
Abbi plays the best as a far-out field,
Winning the game meant that we were the best.
We all cracked a smile as we raised the shield
OLSC is better than the rest.
We knew the medal was ours in the end,
And so we broke the Codsall's winning trend.

Laura Corbett (15)
Our Lady & St Chad Catholic School, Wolverhampton

Greed

When summer is here,
I long for the cold of winter,
To cool down the heat.

And when winter arrives,
I long for the extreme heat,
Of the warm summer.

When it rains heavily,
I long for the dry again,
To dry my clothes off.

Though if it is dry,
I long for the rain and damp
To quench my thirst.

I always long for
What I cannot have right now,
I am known as Greed!

Daniel Love (12)
Our Lady & St Chad Catholic School, Wolverhampton

A Girl Who's Lost In The World Of Racism

My question is why are we different?
We all have eyes, we all have ears, why judge?
I feel isolated, but I'm tolerant
My heart burns of fear, why hold a grudge?
I try, I try, I try, you know I try
You do know I suffer, inside I burn
I cry, I cry, I cry, you know I cry
Why be racist, why don't we all just learn?
The question I ask, is why be blatant?
Racism is not the answer, why do it?
I feel small, I am not confident
Are you trying to make a point? Prove it!
Why cause trauma, why cause pain and drama?
What goes around will come back as bad karma!

Thandiwe Mandimutsira (15)
Our Lady & St Chad Catholic School, Wolverhampton

Imagine . . .

The sun was shining upon the palm trees
Cold water was glistening in the breeze
Golden-brown sand was burning with its might
The air was cooling everyone in sight
The children watched the splashes in the sea
Children sing around, we are so happy!
Children are making enchanting castles
Sand making jungles where snakes do rattle.
Seashells from the sea for the hard-knock ground
Rotted old fossils that were never found
In reality they know it is true
The things they think of, you wish it was you.
As you can see a bud in a flower
The flower uplifts within an hour.

Priscilla Hamilton (13)
Our Lady & St Chad Catholic School, Wolverhampton

My Thing . . .

They're tiny, they're small, they're big, they're large,
Size doesn't matter just get on your board,
Ride with thrill and the adrenaline rush,
People are staring, no need to blush.

The sun, the sand
The board under your hand
The thrill, the skill
As well as the will.

Love it, like it, hate it, don't
Just ride the waves
Give what you've got.

Keep fit, get wet, have fun not glum
You swim, you dive, you also run.

The hobby, the sport, the thing that I do
It's called surfing, what about you?

Kelly Gilbert (15)
Our Lady & St Chad Catholic School, Wolverhampton

No Words Describe You

There are no words to describe you
You shine like the sun and glitter like the sea,
You shine like Heaven, like God shines on me,
You take my sorrow and it makes me hollow.

You look like the moon, but shining like a spoon,
Your name is Chelsea, like the team I love,
You shine like a dove, right into my love,
Your hair is so brown like melted chocolate,
You're so fair and as cute as a little hare.

Ben Cox (13) & Dayl Harding (12)
Our Lady & St Chad Catholic School, Wolverhampton

What Love Does . . .

Absence makes the heart grow fonder,
At least that's what they say,
But they don't know the pain I feel,
Missing you more each day.

Time apart is time to think,
And that's just what I need,
At least that's what I tell myself,
When really, my heart bleeds.

When I stop and think too long,
Of what we used to share,
My eyes well up and my heart pains,
And I know I still care.

I try my best to shrug it off,
And tell myself I'm stronger,
But it's been inside my heart too long,
It's bound to stay for longer.

This is my chance to let it go,
To set my feelings free,
But I can't help what love does
And it's got a hold of me.

Kirsty Gay (14)
Our Lady & St Chad Catholic School, Wolverhampton

Hollow

Miles of land, but none to
Sew seeds, seas of water
But nothing to drink
Millions of people, none of
Them bleed, no glory,
No innocence . . .
Nothing

For Africa.

Apolloniah Dunkley (15)
Our Lady & St Chad Catholic School, Wolverhampton

Sun, Stars, Air And The Shadowed Moon

You're the sun, stars, air and the shadowed moon,
Your face glitters at exactly twelve noon,
Heavens above worship your darling love,
Your heart is cushioned in a secret glove.

Singing, clapping, using all the senses,
Angels from Heaven come to say the best,
They agree with our love now and forever,
Through time and space we'll be together.

Your voice is music, music to my ears,
Flowers, golden doves, bringing you to tears,
You're the best thing that has ever happened,
We will be together forever more.

Thomas Illingworth (13)
Our Lady & St Chad Catholic School, Wolverhampton

XXCI

(Inspired by Shakespeare's Sonnets)

I will compare you to a winter's night,
You are more volatile and more sour,
The winter winds execute the darling buds of May,
And winter's lease is long and lasting,
Sometimes too cold the eye of Heaven fades,
And always her complexion dimmed,
And everything that is good always declines,
By chance or sometimes on purpose
But your eternal winter will never fade,
Or lose possession of the bitterness you own,
Death brags of your constant presence in his shade,
When time passes you by too quickly.
So long as men live and look upon you
Your poison will drain the life from them too.

Emma Allen (14)
Our Lady & St Chad Catholic School, Wolverhampton

Love

(Inspired by Shakespeare)

Roses are red, violets are blue, sugar
Is sweet, not as sweet as my darling you,
If love was a flower you'd be my rose,
Your skin is like silk, your eyes are like gold.
There are no words that describe you my love,
You are the moon, sun and the shining stars,
Your face lights up my day when I see you,
You shine like the sun, Earth and the heavens,
The bells start to ring loud as your voice sings,
The way you sing makes the birds fly so high,
You sing like an angel up in Heaven,
You belong in Heaven, my darling you,
The way you sing is the way I cheer,
I can now have a cold pint of beer!

Thomas Pearce (13)
Our Lady & St Chad Catholic School, Wolverhampton

The Beautiful Day

A light, airy breeze blew through the tall trees,
All the animals out, including the bees,
Refreshing rivers running over the hills,
Everywhere you look there are windmills!

The cool, clear, clean, relaxing atmosphere,
Countryside parks filled with newborn deer,
Water glistens in the shining sunlight,
People are rid of all signs of fear and fright.

Lakes ripple as pebbles are thrown in,
People's faces filled with gigantic grins,
A man in the park is walking his pet dog,
A little girl sat on a hedgehog . . .
> *Ouch!*

Chelsea Evans (12)
Our Lady & St Chad Catholic School, Wolverhampton

My Magic Box

(Inspired by 'Magic Box' by Kit Wright)

I will treasure in my box . . .

A picture of my mother as a child,
A touch of a snowman with his ice-cold fingers,
The smell of McDonald's drifting through the air,
And the smell of flowers that make a lovely scent.

I will place in my box . . .

The laughter of my family when I say something funny,
A video of me growing up . . .
A picture of my family when we went to Wales,
And the fresh air that makex the trees go *swoosh!*

I will add in my box . . .

My mom and dad's laughter
A riddle from the old ages
The sound of the fireworks going, *'Boom, bang,'*
And the picture of my sister screaming on a scary ride.

My box is gold with silver hinges,
In my box I will sail for a day or two,
Then dig for gold until the sun goes down.

Alana Clarke McDonald (12)
Our Lady & St Chad Catholic School, Wolverhampton

The Four Wonders

The summer sun crackling in the air,
Not too hot or cold to bare,
With flowers blooming like a person growing up,
With the smell so sweet like a buttercup,
People bathing in their ice-cold pool,
Enjoy a good breeze which is cold and cool.

As cool as winter, cold as can be
White snow and ice is all you can see,
Like a white ghost snow lies still,
Snow will amaze you, I know it will.

Amazing autumn leaves are falling,
Orange, red and brown.
See them twirling in the wind,
And floating to the ground.

Springtime's here the last I will say,
But it's great to get up to a lovely spring day
You'll see baby lambs cute as can be,
Spring is a season you'll have to see.

Joseph Smith (12)
Our Lady & St Chad Catholic School, Wolverhampton

Poem

I do not want to write a poem,
It makes me want to run straight home.

When I try to find two words to rhyme,
I'm always stressed about running out of time.

It makes me angry like the hulk
So I just start to sulk

My pencil groans when I write a line,
When someone questions me about the poem I sadly say, 'It's mine.'

I start to go in a rage,
I'm getting furious, so I yank out the page.

I start again to find something to write about,
I've had my hand up for ages, so I start to shout.

I'm trying my hardest to write a poem,
I feel like I have the knowledge of a garden gnome.

In all the excitement I realise I've just written a poem,
Now all I have to do is write something that rhymes,
That word is 'foam'.

Rickeno Heera (12)
Our Lady & St Chad Catholic School, Wolverhampton

Not A Clue

Why? Why do people kick me?
Smash me up in the air.
Play with me for ninety minutes
And keep me under the chair.

Why? Why do people throw me?
Throw me over the line.
Throw me towards the manager,
Who is drinking a glass of wine.

Why? Why do people love me?
Praise me before a match.
The home team love my tough leather,
When the keeper makes a catch.

Why? Why am I round?
Floating across the floor
I love my smooth body
I am worth twenty pound.

What am I?
Football.

Kevin McGloin (12)
Our Lady & St Chad Catholic School, Wolverhampton

Powerless . . .

The world has cried so many tears
Family and friends have been lost over the years.
So much hurt in the world today
All this suffering and pain doesn't seem to go away,
I begin to wonder if it ever will
Terrorists diminishing lives just to get a thrill!
Will Africa ever get to eat?
Or should we just admit defeat?
The world is falling apart before my eyes
And all I can do is walk on by . . .

Hannah Mole (15)
Our Lady & St Chad Catholic School, Wolverhampton

God Bless

Even if your life is hard
Put your faith in God
Believe in yourself 'cause you're a strong believer
Don't be tempted by the Devil because he's a strong deceiver
Even if you have rivals
Believe in the Father and keep reading the Bible
When I die, I wouldn't worry about the life after
As long as I read all the chapters.

I've seen all the pain and glory
Listen to my life story
Ever since birth
I've always gone to church
It was hard for me to be a beginner in Christ
Later on I became a sinner in life
But still I didn't impress my parents
When they weren't around the house I'd be swearing
When I was a teenager I thought I saw perfection
Because sin had me caught up and was tempting
I never knew the direction.
When I realised I'd sinned, I needed advice
Somebody told me about God and on that day I started a new life.
I'm now a new person and with God I ain't a victim
'Cause now I'm a Christian.

Even if your life gets harder
Trust in the heavenly father
Even if you're going through stress
God is going to get you blessed.

Brighton Ndlovu (15)
Our Lady & St Chad Catholic School, Wolverhampton

Life Still Has A Meaning

When the day is dull, and the night is bright
When the shining sky shows the sun beaming
Watching the roses close, feeling wrong not right,
Remember, life still has a meaning.
Behind the scenes, is what you can't see,
Under the living nothing is steaming.
An unknown vision waiting to be seen,
Though the heart's deep, and hurt you are feeling
With each taken blink, soft and very clean,
You wonder if life still has a meaning?
When the flowers restore, people are keen
As the earth is loved, filled with great healing
Then life is released, many are feeling
They can see that life still has a meaning . . .

Soju Tyra Ademiluyi (15)
Our Lady & St Chad Catholic School, Wolverhampton

Casting All My Burdens Unto Him

God when I trip, You do not break my fall
God I'm always mocked, I cannot walk tall
God they judge me, they do not know my soul
God in grief, my feelings I cannot show
God they hurt me, why I do not even know
God my heart aches, will they aid me to grow?
God cover me, wrap me Up in Your shawl
God I curse, stress is taking its toll
God I'm faithless, I'm down, I am so low
God I bang my head against a brick wall
God I yearn for You, I beg *hear my call*
God leave this wicked place once and for all
God will I overcome, will I shine and glow?
My scattered blood forever it will flow.

Chenai Zamangwe (15)
Our Lady & St Chad Catholic School, Wolverhampton

Just Tell Me Why

You said you loved me so,
There's so many things you need to know,
You made me laugh, you made me cry,
Just let me know, just tell me why.

As love struck me down,
God must have sent me an angel,
From the heavens above,
To heal this broken heart of mine,
From being in love.

You left without saying goodbye
I sit there daydreaming, wondering *why?*
The good times, the bad times,
They're what makes you mine
No doubt, I will love you for all my time.

But as we're growing older,
I'm starting to see sense,
The longer we're apart, the more I need you here
To make me complete, to make me happy,
To wash away all my fears.

I know things may be different now,
But I will always love you so,
Just let me know, just tell me why
You broke my heart, I know.

Alice Vaughan (15)
Our Lady & St Chad Catholic School, Wolverhampton

Summertime

Slapping on the suncream,
Blowing up the rubber ring,
Packing all the towels,
And polishing my sunglasses.

Walking down the hill,
Getting hot and sweaty
Dreaming of that moment,
When you dig your big toe in.

Finally we've got there,
Onto the sand,
Feeling it beneath your feet
And it tickling your toes.

Setting up camp in the middle of the beach,
Picking up the rubber ring
Running to the sea
Dodging all the crabs.

Here it goes
1, 2, 3,
Putting in my big toe
And pull it out again.

Ouch,
It's freezing,
I'll have another go,
In go both my feet.

Now my arms are in,
Next I put my head in,
And swim a bit like a fish.
I climb upon my rubber ring.

I am lying there happily when,
Splash!
They've pushed me in!

Eleanor Davis (13)
St Dominic's Priory School, Stone

Packing

Tomorrow we're off on our holidays,
We're jetting off to the sun.
We're going to glorious Spain,
Oh I hope we'll get there in time.

My family is so unorganised,
There's a ton of things to pack.
There's a list as long as a railway track,
Oh I hope we'll get there in time.

My mum and dad have just started,
With an hour until we've got to leave.
You don't even want to know what my sister's doing,
Oh I hope we'll get there in time.

With half an hour to spare,
We've still got to catch the dog,
I think I've just seen her running off,
Oh I hope we'll get there in time.

We're throwing the luggage into the car,
Remembering all we can.
Mum's forgotten the car keys,
Oh I hope we'll get there in time.

We're racing down the motorway,
Dad's swearing at the cars.
We run into the terminal,
We've made it just in time.

Abigail Price (13)
St Dominic's Priory School, Stone

Baptised In Acid

Baptised in acid, a placid kiss soaks in my veins
Reminding me of Heaven yet tripping over its remains
It leads me to a meadow of unyielding blades
With a sunset cast behind it, and a hint of purple haze
Sliding down a razor, slitting wrists on this playground
Conveyed a bloody image of an angel who's dreams were never found
The sky became an ocean swimming with dead corpses
Remorse was their cries as I joined their evil forces
Waves of raged refugees came crashing to their knees
For I was their leader, they once had followed me
Swallowed seeds of betrayal left a trail of calamity
The sanity was lost and my world had vanished from thee
Banished from my soul for you had held the key
The cage that held our future - we now walk upon debris.

Kallum Beattie (15)
St Edmund's Catholic School, Wolverhampton

The Mighty Oak Tree

There lived a boy in Edinburgh
And no known friends had he
For his dearest and only friend
Was the mighty oak tree.
All through the day the boy would dream
Of the oak's open arms
And resting there he felt at peace
Away from all world's harms.
Not only did he feel at rest
He talked to the tree too
About his problems and his thoughts
It stopped him feeling blue
He once tried to talk to someone
They did not understand
Of all the questions the boy asked
The answers were all bland.
Then one day in December morn
The tree was snatched away
And the boy left sad and helpless
Could not help feeling grey
The mother seeing the boy's gloom
Went with him to the woods
And found the perfect shaped acorn
Planted it amongst buds
The acorn did then grow and grow
With that the boy as well
Feeling the oak and himself thrive
Made him come out his shell.

Patrick Ward (12)
St John Houghton Catholic School, Ilkeston

Tsunami Aftermath

Helpless am I,
Why I cannot die,
I don't know,
My son is dying
They should be flying
The black crows.

On my own,
Myself, alone.

Sun beating down
I look around
Just rubble,
A leg I see,
Could it now be
Just rubble.

On my own,
Myself, alone.

A gasp of breath,
Some hope is left
My child I see
A lot of glee
Consumes me.

Through whatever
We're together.

Callan Durrant (12)
St Peter's CE (A) High School, Stoke-on-Trent

Stoke-On-Trent

The kilns that stood
So proud, so tall
Submitted to the wrecking ball
Fell victim to the modern ways
We're longing for the good old days.

So now there is
No more demand
For vases from the potters hand
Machines now mould over precious clays
We're longing for the good old days.

Well I suppose
The future's set,
But then at least they won't forget
About the oven's burning blaze
But we're longing for the good old days.

Oh well I guess,
We'll have to learn
All of these men with cash to burn
'Convenience' is what he says
Is he longing for the good old days?

Katherine Vaughan (12)
St Peter's CE (A) High School, Stoke-on-Trent

Friends

F riends can come from different places
R ich, poor or different races
 I n every friend there is a different quality
E xciting, kind, funny or loving
N o friend can be the same
D umb, clever or even lame
S o don't disrespect your friends and you can keep them forever.

Chloe Dykes (12)
St Peter's CE (A) High School, Stoke-on-Trent

Stoke-On-Trent

Stoke-on-Trent is really great,
It's just the place to be,
So come on in and don't be late
There's so much to do and see.

Stoke-on-Trent used to be,
Full of industry.
They've nearly all gone but there's still some to see,
It's not that bad really.

There are pictures and pots and lots of shops
And oatcakes for your tea.
There's Signal 1 with Top of the Pops
And football grounds to see.

Visit our museums, look and learn
What Stoke-on-Trent has to offer
Coal, canals and some church bells
It's great to be a potter.

Robyn Tunnicliff (12)
St Peter's CE (A) High School, Stoke-on-Trent

My Poem!

Boyfriends come
And boyfriends go
Why don't they stay?
I'll never know
Do you?

Rebecca Williams (12)
St Peter's CE (A) High School, Stoke-on-Trent

Litter

Don't pollute our environment,
It's not fair,
Nobody's listening,
Why don't you care?

If you have got some litter,
Don't chuck it on the ground,
Or else you will pollute our environment,
And there will be litter all around.

Litter pollutes our environment,
You might think litter is cool,
It's not, believe me,
So don't be a fool!

Bin your litter!

Lisa Cotton (12)
St Peter's CE (A) High School, Stoke-on-Trent

Tsunami Kennings

Land sweeper
Water deeper
Human killer
Chaos bringer
City soaker
Child choker
Tidal wave
Giant grave
Tree ripper
Headline gripper
Thirty feeter
Human eater
Earth shaker
History maker.

Sam Frawley (12)
St Peter's CE (A) High School, Stoke-on-Trent

Killer Alien

I'm an alien and I'm the best;
I'm cleverer than you and all the rest.
I'll take over France, and I'll take over Spain,
And then I'll have a nice, long reign.

I'm just so brave, and I'm really cool;
I was born with brains and I don't go to school
So clear off humans, save your lives;
Or I'll roast your brains in pickle and chives.

I'm sitting here, in a cool disguise,
And I'm here just to pulverise.
I'm the best, so hear me out:
I'm the king, and I'll wipe you out.

I ate your bones, and I crunched your tongue
I waited for this moment for so long.
This is the end and I've done what I say,
Pack it in humans; it's nice this way.

Sumayah Bukhari (13)
St Peter's CE (A) High School, Stoke-on-Trent

Fairies

Fairies are magical creatures
They have loads of different features
Fairies have wings and wands
They live by the delicates of all ponds
Fairies can grant your every wish
Including your favourite food dish
They are a mystery to everybody
Fairies are not all that easy to find like cartoon Noddy.

Láuren Parsons (12)
St Peter's CE (A) High School, Stoke-on-Trent

The Sands Of My Time

As I sit here, I know,
That the sand grains do drop
And my time becomes less,
But I find that my knowledge is more.

Yet I find in that time,
I ask myself different questions
Questions of time and space and of mind
In each a tiresome way.

When will I know the things that I own,
Are nothing to those that be
And my life has a time
And the sand grains still fall.

The things I have found,
Are changing my mind
I know not of wishes and dreams or
The well of fate and the penny of luck.

They only hinder my time,
The grit of the grain is no less
And the hourglass is running me out
To nothing except my mind.

Sylvina Richardson (14)
St Peter's CE (A) High School, Stoke-on-Trent

Animals

Jungle, forest, ocean, everywhere!
Animals are here and there,
Monkeys, pigs, birds, fish, cow
Some animals just make you say wow!
Big, scary, dangerous, tall,
Weird, amazing small!
Predators, consumers, prey
Animals are here to stay!

Louise Sherwin (12)
St Peter's CE (A) High School, Stoke-on-Trent

The Painting Of My True Fear . . .

The painting of my true fear . . .
Is a black hole filled with no emotion,
A tunnel without a light at the end
Where the future appears bleak and doomed.

The painting of my true fear . . .
Is an animal killing a soul,
Ripping the flesh and tearing the spirit,
Destroying a precious life.

The painting of my true fear . . .
Is a world where people kill or be killed,
Where happiness is a myth
And depression is a reality.

The painting of my true fear . . .
Is a broken heart unable to mend,
Being slashed by a knife so many times,
That it can no longer live life at all.

The painting of my true fear . . .
Is where love is just a game,
Only to be played by the clever
Who are too stupid to know they will never win.

The painting of my true fear . . .
Is a picture with faded colour,
The painting of my true fear . . .
Is a picture without you in it.

Hannah-Marie Lund (14)
St Peter's CE (A) High School, Stoke-on-Trent

My Dream

I have a dream,
But you'll probably laugh,
But I think that I have the confidence
I know you'll think it sounds daft!

I want to become famous, and it doesn't matter how
Like, Jennifer Aniston, Britney Spears
I want to be them now.

Wouldn't you just love to walk along the red carpet?
And beside you Brad Pitt or Orlando Bloom
And then you do a cheesy smile for a photo shot!
Now for the after show party you walk into the room.

You look around and see,
Beyoncé performing in front of your very own eyes
You start to dance then realise,
Your making such a fool so you stop and sit down.

On your left is Peter Kay
Cracking you up so much you bellow out a laugh and your white wine
Accidentally comes out to but all over another one of
Shane Ritchie's shirts!

He goes to the toilet,
You go red
And move away
From Peter Kay!

I'd love to be my dream
But it's so hard to do
Well I must admit I'm fine as I am
But it's nice to try something new!

Jade Washington (12)
St Peter's CE (A) High School, Stoke-on-Trent

The Giant

How tiny things appear to a towering giant
Must mighty things appear!
An ocean like a puddle, its waves like little ripples.
A cathedral like a cottage,
A mountain like a mole hill,
The tallest trees within the forest like
Some big sticks
A jumbo jet, a toy plane,
A lake a tear drop
And skyscrapers that touch the stars, a miniature village
In a vase.

Rebecca Tunnicliff (12)
St Peter's CE (A) High School, Stoke-on-Trent

Me And The Next Level

I am happy and sad little thing,
And when I have something great, I just go ding.
But there is another level,
That is commanded by the Devil
And I don't know what to do.

This Oother level, that I describe,
I tell you never subscribe.
But if you do, quick as a fly get out,
I tell you this without a doubt.

But there is hope yet,
You can repay your debt.
Just be happy not sad,
Don't be angry be glad.
When you have achieved, this stage,
In your life, you will turn a new page.

Natasha Hill (14)
St Peter's CE (A) High School, Stoke-on-Trent

Mrs Kelmet

Mrs Kelmet
In her helmet
Riding in the dark
Rode upon a duckling's beak,
And made the duckling squawk.
Mrs Kelmet,
In her helmet,
Let the duckling free,
By lifting up her handlebar
And taking out the key.

Charlotte Rhead (12)
St Peter's CE (A) High School, Stoke-on-Trent

Around The World

The world goes round,
Years go by
24/7 little babies cry.

Children growing up,
People getting old.
We're very young now,
But soon we'll be old.

Look at us we've got more,
Look at them they're very poor,
We've got clean water,
And food to eat.
They're very hungry and need something to eat.

It's time for me to go now,
To go and do my bit,
To go and help the others that are very sick,
If we all work together,
And do our little bit,
Not so many people would be sick.

Jemma Cherry (12)
Sidney Stringer School, Coventry

Different Land

Come with me and take my hand
I'll take you to a different land,
Full of hope, peace and glory and
Bless the Lord as he stands before thee.

Now close your eyes and don't be scared,
You don't really need to come prepared,
While I take you to this different land,
I'll stay with you and hold your hand.

For where we're going the sky is blue
And the flowers are covered with a small residue
For when you left I lost my soul
And now it's left a big black hole.

So when, where or why I hear you cry,
It brings back to me the best times we had.
So whenever you need to have some peace,
Just think of me and that different land
And then someone else, some day, might understand.

Kelly McBride (12)
Sidney Stringer School, Coventry

The Albatross

Soaring, high above the scavenging gulls,
Regal, proud and large.
Out to sea for weeks at a time,
Resting only on the wind.
An amazing quest from land to sea,
Catching fish in harmony.
Riding the wind currents to where they end,
Gliding on pearly, feathered wings.
A hero's welcome it should receive,
As it returns to breed and leave.

Leun Gwynne (13)
The Bishop of Hereford's Bluecoat School, Tupsley

My Bad Deed

On that day many years ago,
We went to the post office.
I was but a small child,
And was keen to prove myself

So in we went through the door,
A dog sitting quietly on the floor.
My mum went to get the things,
While I looked at the toys.

And I took a pair of toy handcuffs,
And hid them under my coat,
So out we went and then back in again,
When Mum saw my theft.

It was alright after that,
The shopkeeper took pity on me,
And told me not to do it again.
Which is exactly what I did from then.

Peter Challenger (14)
The Bishop of Hereford's Bluecoat School, Tupsley

Stars At Night In Hell

To other people stars are great
A twinkle in the sky
A remedy for feeling good
As viewers pass on by.

To me they are a demon
Sitting up on high
Looking pretty and sparkling
As the night trudges by.

They are always in my nightmares
Laughing and looking sly
If only you knew my night
You would probably die.

Tom Whitcombe (14)
The Bishop of Hereford's Bluecoat School, Tupsley

A Poem About Things That Bother Me

Many things have bothered me,
More as I get older,
But the most confusing one of all,
Is other people's feelings.

Secrets, love and friendship,
Make us who we are,
Some change and others stick,
But they're always powerful.

My life has become a secret,
My feelings are unknown,
Only a few truly know me,
And others think they do.

I never got the chance,
To say goodbye to Dan,
He was a great neighbour, even though
He was no relation of mine.

When a girl found out a secret,
So important to me,
I felt like a betrayer,
That I'd betrayed my friend and me.

My life used to be a crystal,
It was clear and hid nothing,
But now it has a dark shadow
That haunts everything.

Even though these things
Have always bothered me,
I know that they were for the best,
They made me who I am.

And that is why they bother me!

Emily Hurdidge (14)
The Bishop of Hereford's Bluecoat School, Tupsley

I Wish!

I wish I was big then I would understand
Understand how this world works
Understand about being small
But I guess I can't, not yet anyway
I wish I could escape anywhere, any day.

I wish I could hold the world in my fist
I would hold it tight all day and all night
I would not let it go until I was ready,
Ready to go to the big land that's heavy.

I wish I was free,
Free to go anywhere I wish
I'd go to a place with not a single lie
And I'll wish and wish until the day I die.

Marnie Ferris (12)
The Bishop of Hereford's Bluecoat School, Tupsley

My First Day Of School

The fire alarm was off and ringing
While I was there just standing and screaming
My favourite teacher was holding my hand
Her skin was as rubbery as a rubber band
The taste of salt was very sickly
And that's the strangest part of this memory
The tears were now missing from my eyes
I felt as though I was saying my goodbyes.

A strong smell of fear was very clear,
And suddenly I felt unwell
I could hear a loud ringing in my ear
This was my first experience of the fire bell.

Nathan Budd (14)
The Chase Technology College, Malvern

Tears At Nursery

Riding round on the tricycle
On the floor as hard as stone.

Suddenly I wobble,
Like a nervous gymnast on a beam.

Then I fall

The blood rushes out of my knee,
Like water running down a river.

I jump up and run inside,
Tears falling down my face, as salty as the sea.

I run and run,
Straight through the front doors.

'Mum, Mum.'

Then I'm grabbed,
Like a bargain in a shop.

'Come in and we'll clean you up,'
her voice as soothing as a hot bath.

Emily Morris (13)
The Chase Technology College, Malvern

My Arrival At Nursery

As I grasped my mum's hand,
Tears rolled down my face,
Pale as a ghost.

The gate slammed shut,
The grey door loomed,
As dull as the sky.

The lady stood waiting,
My heart started racing,
I hid behind my mum,
Like an animal would from its prey.

Elizabeth Humphreys (14)
The Chase Technology College, Malvern

The New Girl

Preened dolls
Perfecting their looks
Wannabes look on
Admiringly
Nervous laughter
Ringing from classrooms
Amazement
At calculator sums and
Baffling chess moves
Drugged up fools
Ducking and diving
Behind the bike sheds
Discussing new suppliers
Unfazed, gormless
Looks on their faces
Chilled out guys and gals
Idling in the sun
Like fat,
Jiggling caterpillars.
And there you stand
Bewildered, stranded
Oblivious that the next choice you make could
Determine the whole of your teen life.
But rolling around in the back of your mind
Is the well known, denied fact that
People don't like what they don't know -
The new girl.
     'Come and eat with us.'
. . . and that's it,
Your life decided for you.

Harriet Lloyd (13)
The Chase Technology College, Malvern

My Memory

Waiting for everyone,
Like someone waiting for a kettle to boil.
Waiting,
Like a mother waiting for a child to do up their shoes.
Waiting,
Like a person waiting for their SATs results.
Waiting,
Like waiting for a birthday.
Finally, we go
The excitement starting to kick in,
As if it was Christmas happening all over again.
All the children laughing and talking,
As if it was the start of a new, exciting adventure.
I felt a taste of anxiety in my mouth,
As if I was just about to go on a roller coaster.

We're here - *yippee!*
It may only be down the road
But it took forever and was very hot too,
It was like walking across the Sahara Desert!

I heard a dog whining at a closed door,
Like a seal yelping when it's about to be fed.
Then we went quiet,
And our full attention was on the trip,
Like a sergeant marching their army.

The trip was quick,
And went by like a flash of lightning.
However, it was very interesting,
Like watching a chimpanzee live in the wild.

Claire Riley (14)
The Chase Technology College, Malvern

All Childhood Is A Joke

The greatest dream a child ever had,
Was to become big like their mum and dad.
Eat as much ice cream as they see fit,
Stay up till ten o'clock, watching Crimewatch.
You could drive your own car, go to the pub,
You could have a wallet with lots of money,
Spend it on every new video game in the shop,
And not have to go to school.

But all childhood is a joke,
You have to be indoors before seven,
Eat your vegetables, drink your glass of water,
No ice cream for afters, just an empty stomach,
No fizzy cola, chips or pizza,
Just a boring plate of spinach,
Mashed potatoes and gravy.
Up to bed by 8 o'clock
And dreadful school the next morning.

Your mother packs your lunchbox,
Cheese sandwich, fruit bar, apple juice and an orange,
Your best mate gets to eat tubs of jelly,
And while you're drinking your juice carton,
He slurps a can of lemonade,
Leaving me hot and stuffy,
Your teacher jabbers on about equations,
You fall asleep, and dream about becoming an adult.

Oliver Hall   (14)
The Chase Technology College, Malvern

The Day I Left My Parents For The First Time

The noise was like a birthday party
The sight of happy faces, smiling and laughing
As I played with all the new toys with excitement.

The taste of my breakfast as I entered the room
The mixed smell of paint and plasticine made me feel sick
As I was full and excited.

The way the sand felt as it tickled through my fingers
As part of the sand stuck to my fingers
Like glue and started to itch as it lingered on my skin.

Tamsyn Smith (14)
The Chase Technology College, Malvern

Mother Leaves Me

It's the first time I've been away from Mum
I don't know anyone and I feel all alone.
I just want to cry, or not feel so scared,
Then I see my mum walk through the door.

When it's snack time I feel much better,
Crisps, milk and having people to look after me
Is as comforting as a soft pillow.

Although the smell of tea and coffee seems to
Make me feel as far away from home
As the moon.

Overwhelmed by the shouts and screams
Erupting from the hall like a volcano.

Sebastian Edwards (14)
The Chase Technology College, Malvern

Childhood Is Limitless

Childhood is limitless, for some it is infinite
Childhood can also be short, for those who enjoy it
Childhood can be a loop, of the same routine every day,
And as you grow into adulthood
You see the fun you've left behind.

Some people think it ends when you reach eighteen,
Some people think it ends after high school,
Some people don't think it ends at all,
And some people don't even find the beginning.

Childhood can be the best part of your life,
Childhood can be the only fun time you have
Childhood can be the time for you to not care
Childhood can be the most important time of all.

Richard Fuller (14)
The Chase Technology College, Malvern

Go Home!

Zoom, zoom, zooming around the room
All you could hear was *scream, scream!*
Little kids wishing they could
Go home, go home!

When I saw my mum drive away,
I was scared I would never see her again,
I wished I could
Go home, go home!

I could smell the burning from the kitchen,
I hated it, it was like a forest was burning,
All of the stuff wished they could
Go home, go home!

Niall Phillips (14)
The Chase Technology College, Malvern

First Day

I remember my first day,
I remember the summer breeze
I remember the sea of chatter
Of children and parents
Screaming and comforting.

I remember my oldest friend,
Greeting me for the first time,
Asking his mum,
If he could speak to a stranger
And a nod of reassurance.

I remember the first lesson,
A hoarse voice,
Stern and straight,
Telling us our parents aren't gone,
But the kicking and screaming continued.

I remember the yells of delight,
As my first playtime began,
And a game of tag began,
And my life at school began . . .
I remember well.

Troy Tittley (14)
The Chase Technology College, Malvern

Childhood Is A Memory

Childhood is a memory
It either goes on forever or
It stops and starts
Or it never begins.

Everyone finally grows up
They remember every detail
Or they try to forget the entire experience.

Childhood can be tormenting, lonely and unpredictable,
On the other hand, it can be enjoyable,
Interesting and different on every day.

The most important thing to remember
Is that you only have one chance in childhood,
And you should cherish every moment.

Stuart Davison (14)
The Chase Technology College, Malvern

Playground Memories

The noise was as loud as a plane landing, carrying a lot
                                        of angry passengers.
The smell of the wet sand was as overpowering as petrol
                                        on a hot day.
The taste of the drink I had on the way there,
Was as tangy as a Jaffa Cake.
The sight of seeing what I had done was like standing trial
                                        for a crime.
The touch of the wet sand was as gritty and wet as grit salt
                                        on a wet road.

Rebecca Cook (14)
The Chase Technology College, Malvern

The Stranger Niece

Lost inside just like a poor, orphaned child
Trapped in a dark wood of bewilderment
Try to stay calm, feel only feelings mild
For a plastic heart is one only lent
A blanketed body, a stranger niece
An image of the child I should've met
A slice of heart, one broken shattered piece
Salt on my lips, tears painting my cheeks wet
Cheeks themselves red, scarlet, rose-petal red,
You cry inside so as not to destroy Mum
But it's hard to get her out of your head
That sweet baby girl, Erin Elysia
So you hang tight to that sprinkle of hope,
Even though it's so very hard to cope.

Verity Cary (14)
The Chase Technology College, Malvern

The First Day Of Nursery

Walking through the door which was as arched
As an elephant's trunk.

Holding my mum's hand,
Her skin was as soft as silk.

The children were dressed as bright
As magnesium alight.

The nursery was as loud as a football stadium
Alive with screaming fans.

The taste of tears as salty as the sea.

Jessica Bird (13)
The Chase Technology College, Malvern

Why School Sucks

School is boring,
You know it's true.
Maths, English and science,
You know they are all so dull.
The only subject that might be interesting,
Is art where you can flick paint across the room.
PE is the best subject,
Where you get to play football or rugby.
Maths is rubbish,
You don't even need it in later life.
English really sucks,
All you do is write and learn about writing.
Science is very boring,
Except when your teacher almost blows himself up.
DT's are so boring,
But they fly around all over the place.
I'm ashamed of the government,
Who force us to go to school
If I become someone in power,
I'd change that straight away.
I wish school would go away,
Well it will soon because of the holiday.

Stephen Tyler (14)
The Coventry Blue Coat CE School, Coventry

School

School is a dreary place,
I warn you not to go there.
Primary school is a boring place,
With English, maths and science.
Secondary school is way more fun,
With drama, music and art.
The head teacher just hides himself in his office,
Like a hermit crab in a shell rarely coming out.
The teachers and pupils are on opposite sides,
Battling over uniform or behaviour in the class.
DT's fly everywhere, and pupils disappear to the detention block.
The pupils have wars of their own on the playground,
Over issues like girlfriends or boyfriends,
Or sometimes they just want to start a fight.
The forms are forced to compete against each other,
In PE, sports day and a number of other activities.
The school goes in a big fuss when parents come to look,
They make you work extra hard to impress.
Year 7 is the easiest year and it gets harder through the years,
Though as I said before,
School is a dreary place,
I warn you not to go there.

Joshua Wiffen (14)
The Coventry Blue Coat CE School, Coventry

In Mrs Gould's Class

Cheerful colours, friendly feel,
Familiar desks the same as ever.
Writing about the holiday, no punctuation,
Writing so small Mrs Gould claims
She needs a microscope to read,
But leaves you a star for, just the same.

Going to the pond with hopes high
With expectations of frogs, soon to
Sink again when nothing shows its face.
Playing house, arguing over the
Ironing board, teacups and chairs.
Swimming, maths, English and art.

Laughing with Eleanor and Catherine
Playing hopscotch, tig, stuck in the mud.
Amusing the dinner ladies.
Ants in the lunchboxes
Work to go on the walls
Michael's house for tea, Isla's house to play.

Listening on the carpet at 'tell time',
David's hamster's died, Becky's got a baby cousin.
Elizabeth's leaving
Off to another place of fun, laughter and learning.
The same and entirely different.
Older now and not so innocent
Writing letters, keen at first,
But slowly drifting, drifting away.
Memories slowly fading
But always there.

Elizabeth Hare (13)
The Coventry Blue Coat CE School, Coventry

Book Demons

I've read too many books,
They're confused in my head,
I've got wizards and witches,
And demons and dread.

It's all in my head,
Where I fly,
It's a lie.

I see eagles on cliff tops,
And actors on back drops,
And teachers and preachers,
And mythical creatures,
And here I lie on my bed,
With all of these things in my head.

I stand in my room,
I'm here on my own,
I listen to silence
And pick up the phone.
I call a friend,
They don't pick up,
I'm out of my head,
And I'm down on my luck.

I go to my room,
I lie on the floor,
My head starts to wonder,
The same as before,
I'm dead to the world,
I'm here in my mind,
Just one more lost thing,
For the demons to find.

Amy Wood (14)
The Coventry Blue Coat CE School, Coventry

Mrs Poulter's Class

'Don't worry you're going to be fine here!'
I heard a voice whisper into my ear!
But I didn't think so!
Working on boring white paper,
With the long, slim, sharp pencils,
Too long for me to hold,
Counting numbers very slowly,
Getting confused with each number,
Sitting on the rough green carpet,
Which hurt your hands.
'I'd rather be at home!'
I kept thinking to myself longingly,
The whole school looked so . . . plain!
Creamy walls which looked like whipped cream,
Bookshelves with a mountain of books,
White, boring, hard tables and chairs all in a row!
Children running around and laughing hysterically,
Others shouting at each other angrily, fists clenched!
Others punching and kicking past people harshly!

I looked around bewildered looking down and up!
Until I saw the fascinating rain on the top window!
Falling quickly, tinkling joyfully,
I watched it entranced, smiling,
As they danced on the cold pane of glass!
I looked back on the room, unhappily,
Children scribbled on the blackboard,
Random drawings and scribbles,
With a stubby powdery chalk piece,
Pictures of colourful shapes hung on the wall!
Encircling me with their bright colours,
Making my eyes sting,
And my head spin,
Mrs Poulter walked in with a smile of utmost delight!
Beaming at every single one of them,
Through her rounded glasses!
Everyone walked over to their seats swiftly,
As we started my first lesson in that school!

Michaela Reynolds (13)
The Coventry Blue Coat CE School, Coventry

School

First day of school
Nerves and mixed feelings
Filter through the class.

Miss Johnson stands
At the front of the class.
Trying to start numeracy hour.

The bell rings for break,
The playground starts spinning
With noisy, boisterous children.

'Ding' – the bell rings again.

Hot, sweaty children come in from play,
They rush to change their shoes to slippers,
Then they run to their literacy lesson.

Everyone loves Mr Depp, the literacy teacher
So they are eager to get on with the lesson.
In peace and tranquillity.

In topic lessons we have learnt about
The Tudors and Henry VIII
We learnt a song about his six wives.

Sports day is coming up soon,
I am in the relay team,
I hope Tudor win it again.

Last year Tudor won
We got a big trophy
And celebrated all day long.

As the year goes on
And autumn changes into winter
And winter into spring and summer.

It seems like I've only just begun
When actually year 6 is finishing.

Lauren Bennett (14)
The Coventry Blue Coat CE School, Coventry

Where I Go Is Anyone's Guess!

It's like a game of hide and seek,
Tom will take a glance behind the bin,
Obviously he was nowhere near,
The wind can give a hint of where I am,
Directing its air towards me.
Where'd he go? . . . I hear,
Somewhere close but I'm in the clear.
Maybe, I might change places:
Like a person with many faces.
Tom starts running around,
I must find him he says.
Obviously he wouldn't.
I'm like a ghost's shadow,
Stealth's the idea.
Who said I was cheating?
All someone needs to do is to get some
Light on the dark,
But who was to tell?
That's a big giveaway.
Hiding requires skill,
A simple and clever place,
Somewhere where no one would think of,
Except for me.
In the end everyone would think
Oooooooohhh!
I didn't say there was an end though.
I hope so anyway.
Darkness would grow
As the light flees.
I might see Tom sometime,
When I have a beard!
Now Tom is patient less and less,
Because where I go is anyone's guess!

Chirag Bhatti (14)
The Coventry Blue Coat CE School, Coventry

It's Just Another Day!

It's just another day
No fun, we do not play
ABC like 123
It's just another day.

Classrooms stuffy and damp
Just like a rotten camp
School's a bore just like a chore
It's just another day.

We learn French and German too
The canteen line is such a queue
We try our best, we need a rest
It's just another day.

'I have a dream' - that's what I see
That's what I learn in history
We have our fun, we cannot run
It's just another day.

In geography I cannot see
The point in learning it
I try so hard I'll soon be scared
It's just another day.

It's now the end of the day
We're tired, we did not play
A bus trip home all alone
It's just another day.

Danielle McDaid (14)
The Coventry Blue Coat CE School, Coventry

Snow!

Snow tickling my nose
Making it bright red
Piles and piles mount up.

> When I exit my house and
> Enter the cold forest
> Crisp, crunch, goes the snow beneath my feet.

With my friend we have play fights
Enjoying the snow time
It's already night.

> I wake up the next morning
> The magic is no longer there,
> Fun has disappeared
> It's gloomy now
> It's gloomy now.

Gursharan Kaur (12)
The Nottingham Emmanuel School, Wilford

Summer Holidays

The summer holidays are fun and exciting because there is
No school, no homework and it is warm.

The school holidays let you lie in bed however long you want,
You can wear what you like, no one can tell you off.

In the summer holidays you can eat what you like all of the time,
You can play out with your friends every day.

In the summer holidays you sometimes go on a holiday
For however long you want in the six weeks break

In the summer holidays the
> Kids
>> Rule!

Samantha Waumsley (12)
The Nottingham Emmanuel School, Wilford

Midnight

Midnight's when the vampires come out
Mmmm fresh blood.

Midnight's when the street lights turn on
Bzzzzz

Midnight's when the waves howl at the enchanting moon
Owwwww!

Midnight's when the foxes start hunting
Sniff, sniff

Midnight's when the bats fly around knowing their way

Midnight's when the creepy noises fly around town
Creak, slam, footsteps

Midnight's when the shadows creep around
Blood, bzz, oww, sniff, eek.

Midnight.

Shannon Sharpe (12)
The Nottingham Emmanuel School, Wilford

Summer Fun

When the summer comes about
You can hear all the kids shout
Let's go out to play
Ice cream, BBQs and water too.
Summer is everything I want to do
Summer, summer we love you.
Long summer nights
Out by the stars
Roasting marshmallows and eating candy bars
Summer, summer we love you!

Becky Bowley (12)
The Nottingham Emmanuel School, Wilford

Football Mad

Have you ever been football mad?
For me, it is not just a passing fad.

I adore and worship the Gunners
They have lots of money to buy the runners.

Arsenal, Arsenal I adore Arsenal
Thierry Henry is a part of me.

He scores all the goals
Using the very best of his soul.

I love Highbury, the noise of our fans,
The crowd are all there in the stand.

For me this is magic on Earth
To see my players running on the turf.

Liam Fox (12)
The Nottingham Emmanuel School, Wilford

Drayton Manor

The wind hits you fast,
When you're having a blast.

When you're in the air,
You get cool hair.

You are fastened in tight,
So you're in for a fright.

It started to stop,
At the top of apocalypse.

It came down quick,
I was really sick.

Overall I had a blast,
Now I've got to go back to class.

William Allen (13)
The Summerhill School, Kingswinford

Rugby

Snap! Another broken bone to go with the rest,
Right before the New Zealand test.
Exciting, exhausting and experimenting with life,
In rugby you get bloodier than being cut with a knife.
To be brilliant you need to train up,
You never know you might win the Heineken Cup
The best players hunt in packs like a fox,
When they have finished you could fit in a box
You need a good breakfast like toast,
So you can kick the ball over the post.
Go on, quit that stupid band,
You could be playing for England!

Jarryd Williams (13)
The Summerhill School, Kingswinford

Drinks In General

There are many different types of drinks,
Water, pop, wine and beer,
Some are cheap and some are dear.

Water is bland and wet,
Pop is sweet and fizzy,
Beer puts you in debt
And wine makes you dizzy.

Everyone needs water, it's a vital part of life,
Your son and your daughter,
And even your hubby and wife.

So when you take a sip today,
Remember about your drink,
Don't forget what I told you,
In the poem I've just written!

Rebekah Windmill (13)
The Summerhill School, Kingswinford

Here They Come!

Bang, bang, here they come,
In landing craft, shoot them
Up into balls - kill.

Shoot, guns rattling ammo
Coming in, shells hitting the floor,
Dead birds frightened to death by the shooting.

No! No! More men kill them,
Fire artillery, open fire,
'Yes what a hit!'
'Sir, tanks! Open fire on them now!'
Bang, bang, boom!
The noise of the gunfire rattles my eardrums.

Aaaaaahhhh!
Men falling down like flies.

Dan Farr (13)
The Summerhill School, Kingswinford

Music Poem!

Rock, pop, R 'n' B,
There are many types of music as you see.
Some you like and some you don't,
Like classical for all the older folk.

Most people are into pop,
It's popular and cheerful and makes you wanna bop!

Rock makes you wanna scream,
It makes you wanna shout.
You even dream about it,
That's what it's all about!

Then there is R 'n' B,
It's a lot like rap as you see.
It's cool and hip,
Makes you wanna move your hips!

Kirsty Brummell (13)
The Summerhill School, Kingswinford

My Hero

If they cry, I cry,
If they die, my will to live will die.
No matter what I do,
I know they're not coming back, it's true.

I think of the last words they said,
When I'm lying in my bed,
I want to see them one last time,
I want their body next to mine.

I miss their eyes, smiles and tears,
My love for them will never disappear.
They were always there for me,
And it was my time to be there for them.

I can hear their voices like they're near,
Like a ghost I'll never fear,
I want them to know how much they meant to me,
But one day, somewhere, they're waiting for me.

Never seeing their face,
Or them tying their lace,
Brings a tear to my eye,
How I never got to say goodbye.

As the dull days go by, I want to cry,
But I have to stick my head up high,
You wiped my eyes when I was sad,
You were my hero, you are my dad.

Abigail Malpass (13)
The Summerhill School, Kingswinford

Music

Music makes you want to dance,
It makes you go into a trance.
When you're at a disco,
It makes you go with the flow.

There are different kinds of music,
One of them is pop.
It really gets you in the beat,
And makes you want to bop.

Another type is rock,
And when you play it really loud
All the neighbours do is knock.

Then three is classical,
For the older ones out there.
It's nice and calms you down,
And lets you feel the air.

Out of all the music
That gets you in the groove,
My favourite is R 'n' B
It makes you want to move.

Rebecca Icke (13)
The Summerhill School, Kingswinford

The Tiger

Look at the tiger in the cage
The kids are laughing at its rage
Look at the tiger in the cage
Look at the tiger trying to sleep
All the children wanting it to leap.

Tom Page (13)
The Summerhill School, Kingswinford

Tornado

In this world we do or die,
Watching children start to cry,
What's in the distance starting to appear?
It's a tornado and it's not going to clear.

It's coming my way
All I can do is sit and pray,
Trying to keep calm,
With a picture of my family in my palm.

Everything's blowing away and everywhere,
All I can see is a whirling, flying chair,
Why did it have to happen on holiday?
Please God, I sit and pray.

I feel dizzy, something's hit my head,
I think I may well could be dead,
I can hear the news on TV
'Please God don't let it be me.'

Lots of people have died,
Millions of people have cried,
The youngest girl aged eighteen,
Lays in hospital, we could hear her scream.

Died of shock,
That later morning,
On April 1991
In the city of Andara.

Stacey Doherty (13)
The Summerhill School, Kingswinford

Music

Music is great
It cheers you up when you're not feeling good
There are so many types of music
You just have to find one or two that you like
But once you have found them
Be sure not to lose them.

Pop is good
It makes you want to sing along
It never makes you bored,
Every chord is worthwhile.

Rock is great
It makes you want to stay out late!
Everyone is jumping around
Rock always makes a crowd.

Classical is calming
Calmer than the sea
It's so calm, just like me.

R 'n' B is full of rhythm
It makes you want to get up with them
It never makes you tired
You just want to dance along.

Stephanie Attwood (13)
The Summerhill School, Kingswinford

The Web Of The Night

As I lay in my bed
With thoughts in my head
My eyes start to pull down
Suddenly I awake and my eyes catch an unwelcome guest.

I jolt forward and see
Shadows moving
Light bending
Forming a beast in the middle of the night.

My curtains slide open
The moon spirals sinisterly
A car alarm wails a crescendo
Trickling laughter in the rain.

I hear a snarling,
I see a face in a tree,
Evil's breath frosts the window
While its laughter chills the bone.

I then awake
Birds chirping, sun rising over the hills
But I always remember no one can escape
The fright or the web of the night!

Andrew Edmunds (13)
The Summerhill School, Kingswinford

Missing

M other is crying and sick with worry. Noise all around,
    everybody's in a hurry.
I nfants alone in the dark, feeling scared
    when suddenly she heard a bark.
S obbing is the noise all around when the attention is turned
    to the bark of a hound.
S olitary is the child who is full of fear, but still has faith
    his family are near.
I f only she had never run away
    maybe she would have been happy today.
N othing can be heard, all that is,
    is the whistle of a bird.
G ood will be the moment the moment when she is found,
    all will be happy and all will be sound.

Katy Lewis (13)
The Summerhill School, Kingswinford

Summer

Ice cream, bucket and spade,
Try to stay in the shade
The waves are washing your feet
It cools you in the immense heat.

                Having picnics in the park
                It's ten o'clock and it still isn't dark
                Everybody loves July
                But everybody hates the flies.

Going out with your friends
Water fights never end
Chasing each other, running around
The laughing and shouting is a great sound.

Matthew Veness (13)
The Summerhill School, Kingswinford

Summer

Summertime has come!
As the bright, beautiful sun comes out
Every day like a golden ball;
People are having fun;
People are relaxing in the sun.

The blue, crystal sea glimmers offshore,
White horses' tails gallop
The sea crashes gently onto the golden path,
Children screech with delight
As the ice-cold liquid runs around their feet.

Summertime has ended!
Beaches aren't so crowded.
As the night draws in
The blue, crystal sea goes calm, just like me;
The golden path sways as the wind hits it softly.

Emma Whitehouse (13)
The Summerhill School, Kingswinford

London

All we could hear were bombs going off
Mothers and children screaming
They had lost their hearing
It was so loud it hurt our feelings
I could not bear to open my eyes because I could see
People losing their lives
Glass shattering everywhere
Fire engines taking their place
Water flying everywhere
Just in case.

Corral Chambers (13)
The Summerhill School, Kingswinford

MS

MS is really hard,
I never really took it to heart
My legs feel numb
And my life's a bum
Just because I'm not in a wheelchair
People don't seem to care.

Each day feeling down,
Mad crashing around,
Here's how I spend my day
Honestly, I have to say
My family are behind me all the way,
Out every Friday, having a meal,
But I still have to deal with the problems ahead.
I go to Florida three times a year,
But I still fear,
If I fall down or if I'm not fun,
When I walk I feel like a drunk
So to finish my poem, my life has sunk
So now I was thirty-eight.

James Lloyd-Roberts (13)
The Summerhill School, Kingswinford

Inside Feeling

Sitting on the floor,
Deciding what to do,
Staring at the ceiling,
Then I look at you.

And I'm trying to imagine,
Just how life would be;
If I knew your name,
If you would notice me.

I sigh and I wish,
And I sit on my knees;
I glance at you again,
Then you glance at me.

You look away so sharply,
That I think you're trying to hide,
Could you possibly feel,
The way I do inside?

Charlotte Fairley (12)
The Summerhill School, Kingswinford

Sadness

Tears run down my cheek
The cold, unhappy feelings run through my mind.
Crying, weeping, grieving to myself,
The dark, dull, grey colours of sadness all around.

Cannot escape, cannot run, cannot hide,
Frowning into emptiness,
Nobody around to wipe it all away,
Nobody, nothing, all alone.

I mourn, sniff and feel so cold,
My feelings thriving on only sadness,
I can do nothing at all,
Just hope, hope it will all be gone.

I feel so lonely
I feel so sad,
But then smile to myself,
Thinking of all the happy moments
We had together.

Andrew Green (13)
The Summerhill School, Kingswinford

Anger

Anger can be stored away,
Building up inside,
Or you could lash out in what you do or what you say,
Maybe you run away, trying to hide.

But when you store too long
You become something new,
You become filled with hatred and something dark,
You take everything, maybe me or maybe you.

Anger is more than an emotion,
It's a part of you
It's what balances you out,
Avoiding a commotion.

When you can control it
You're good overall,
You learn to stand on your feet,
You no longer stumble and fall.

Joshua Westwood (13)
The Summerhill School, Kingswinford

Music

Dance to the music
Listen to the sound,
Get on the dance floor,
Spin round, round, round.

There are all kinds of music,
Hip hop or rock,
Whichever you like,
You can dance till you drop!

Everyone likes music,
There's something for all,
You can go to a disco
Or even a ball!

Listen to it in your room
Or even in the car,
Listen to it go boom, boom, boom,
Wherever you are!

This poem is about music,
Just to let you know
I love music,
Now you know!

Danielle Payne (13)
The Summerhill School, Kingswinford

Love

Love is good,
Love can be bad.
It depends how you use it.
It's no good if you just dream and sit.

Love can hurt,
Love can make you do the craziest things
But as long as you try,
There'll be no need to cry.

Love is a strong thing,
Stronger than words.
Love can also break your heart,
Especially when you don't want to part.

Love is a special thing,
Something to make your hearts pounce.
There's always someone out there for you,
As they say, there are plenty of fish in the sea.

Tim Keeler (13)
The Summerhill School, Kingswinford

Football Ambition

There is a scout on the sideline,
Watching every step of mine.
I really want her to ask me to sign,
But first I really need to shine.
My chance to be a footballer could come today,
It's the Cup Final, *hip, hip, hooray!*
We should be playing but there is a delay.
Our midfield player can't make it today.
We're one player down, but the whistle blew
I tried my best, it would have to do,
I ran like the wind, could hear them call,
'Abbie, Abbie, pass me the ball!'
I decided to run with the ball
And just ignore that stupid call!
I ran straight up the left hand line
And with some luck, the goal will be mine.
I could never ask for more
I just needed to prove that I could score,
Even though my ankle was sore.
I shot the ball like never before.
It went up high, across their heads
I'd swerved it wide to hit the nets.
The goalie dived, but couldn't make it,
I'd slammed it in, I'd really made it!
I couldn't believe it, my dream had come true
The crowd was roaring, we were winning by two.
I'd scored my goal and the whistle went
What a fantastic end to a great event!

Abigail Brook (12)
The Summerhill School, Kingswinford